GENIUS AND THE MOBOCRACY

FRANK LLOYD WRIGHT

GENIUS AND THE MOBOCRACY

HORIZON PRESS NEW YORK

PUBLISHER'S NOTE This enlarged edition of *Genius and the Mobocracy* contains, in addition to the thirty-nine drawings by Louis Sullivan from the original edition, two drawings by Frank Lloyd Wright incorporated in the text; a separate section of twenty drawings, nineteen by Louis Sullivan and one by Frank Lloyd Wright, all hitherto unpublished; fifty-four photographs; and two essays by Louis Sullivan on Frank Lloyd Wright's work.

For invaluable help in making available texts and original drawings the publisher wishes to express gratitude to Mrs. Frank Lloyd Wright; to Taliesin members Richard Carney and Bruce Brooks Pfeiffer; and to Adolf K. Placzek, Avery Librarian, Columbia University. The publisher also wishes to thank William Alex and Herbert S. Bailey, Jr., Director of the Princeton University Press, for their advice in discussions of this edition; and Richard Nickel and Aaron Siskind for their kind help in both making the photographs available and supplying the descriptive information about them.

Copyright·© 1949 The Frank Lloyd Wright Foundation

Photographs © 1971 Horizon Press

Library of Congress Catalog Card Number 79-132328

ISBN 0-8180-0022-8

Printed in the United States of America

CONTENTS

LIST OF ILLUSTRATIONS

PREFACE

Time was when architecture was genuine construction, its effects noble because true to causes. The forms were sculptured from materials according to the nature of construction and the life of the time—decorated by indigenous carving and painting. This integrity disappeared among the latter Greeks and the Romans. Time came when Christianity appeared upon the scene and architecture again arose closer to the plastic character of inspired architecture and came alive again for a time. But in the Gothic architecture of the Middle Ages we see the last of architecture as a great style of structure. Gothic architecture approached the organic in character. Sculpture and painting became even more a part of it and music entered it. Then the Renaissance appeared—a rebirth of the ancient forms of Greek and Roman architecture, construction more and more pretended. Features of the old orders of construction like pedestals, pilasters, cornices, and columns, piers and arches or wall masses, domes and pendentives; any effects the architects of that period had seen or now thought impressive were assembled as architecture. Architects proceeded to mix them all up, not according to nature but according to "taste." Instead of creators, architects became operators. All conscientious care for causes disappeared as caution did. Architects now only arranged, composed and the "classic" was soon ready for our inheritance. The laws of creation were not defied because they were not understood but they were not even considered beyond getting whatever picturesque effect architects desired: making the "effects" stick together and stand up.

The picture had now triumphed over architecture, and symbolism took the place of original inspiration.

A certain knowledge of the laws of gravitation was still necessary even for this affair of mere effects, especially if monumental.

But gradually all sense of building as genuine construction became a matter of an inside with independent outer facing to make a picture. The facade, or facing, need have no particular meaning whatever where either interior or purpose were concerned.

For five centuries the great art of architecture, in spite of many earnest attempts at revival, declined.

The Renaissance, in Europe "a setting sun all Europe mistook for dawn," was imported by us to bring our architecture up to the level of a democratic civilization dedicated to freedom. But the spirit of architecture was dead. Human thought had found the printed book. The other arts had fled. Printing was the Machine. In spite of sporadic attempts at "rebirth" by special kinds of abortion, the ancient forms of architecture could only be outraged by the Machine.

Meantime the Machine became the monstrous power that moves us now. All our timely materials like glass and steel came to hand as a great new means of building. But there were no architectural forms suited to their use. The practice of architecture was so far gone to the composer of the picture that we had no architects able to conceive the radical new forms needed to use the new tools and materials with nobility, inspiration, or even intelligence. So our own architects in this new world further falsified symbols and again prostituted the new materials not only by a kind of mimicry but by outrage that made our architecture what it is today—servile, insignificant refuse or puerile nostalgia.

When I speak of architecture as organic I mean the great art of structure coming back to its early integrity: again alive as a great reality.

What forms shall buildings take if the glory of the great edifice is to come back to man again and he be blessed with the great beauty of truth in the way of his life we call his environment: so meretricious, so inappropriate now. How is the sap of human life which we call culture—escaping from autocratic monarchy to democratic freedom—going to establish itself?

It was evident long ago that we must no longer picturize, compose, or in any way pretend. We must conceive and integrate: begin again at the beginning to build the right kind of building in the right way in the right place for the right kind of people. An affair of genius.

Organic architecture is the right answer and the effort to establish it is really what this book is about. Organic building is natural building: construction proceeding harmoniously from the nature of a planned or organized inside outward to a consistent outside.   The space to be lived in is now the human reality of any building and in terms of space we will find the new forms we seek. Or lose them. The old order called "classic" is therefore reversed and where so many of our basic building materials are wholly new, we must search again for the natural way to build buildings appropriate to the unprecedented life now to be lived in them. Our modern advantages should no longer be disadvantageous, as they are.

That we be enamored by the negation brought by the Machine may be inevitable for a time. But I like to imagine this novel negation to be only a platform underfoot to enable a greater splendor of life to be ours than any known to Greek or Roman, Goth or Moor. We should know a life beside which the life they knew would seem not only limited in scale and narrow in range but pale in richness of the color of imagination and integrity of spirit.

As the matter stands, the pallor is ours. The giant leverage the machine might be for human good may fall by its own weight from helpless, human hands, far short of our hope

Spirit only can control it. Spirit is a science mobocracy does not know.

falsifications as we see practiced in the name of art? Wherefore comes this craze on the part of the neophyte to be thought original in character at some master's expense but so willing to settle for a paper "degree" or run for any other short-cut to a job?

The truth is, we need originality more than it was ever needed to make good our claim to democratic freedom. Why can't we be honest about it? If one must steal it—steal it. Take it straight! Why fake it and spoil it?

In any country in any century great individuals like Louis H. Sullivan have been few. Although basic motives (Goethe so reminds us) are but several, the flow of consequential ideas may persist, infinite in variety and great in effect. So, moved by precedent (or trying to get on good terms with themselves), aspiring disciples congregate at the individual font they call MASTER. From mastership precious streams of the "great idea," as they flowed to the master—a temper of his soul—now flow from him to devotees each eager to conduct such small share as he can to little branchlets here and there from which other little twigs by way of other similar diversions meander to little flowers. But no fruit. In any pseudo-civilization such as ours all sap—culture—seems to trickle up and out to inconsequence but dimly conscious, if at all, of the reality that originally sparkled with the vitality of truth—not as a mere mentality but as the temper of a serene and blessed mood: a source. What was with the master a savor of reality in the nature of the man—a quality of his individual self—is an entirely different thing in the hands of the disciple. No longer a reality, it is a ghost. Our environment is haunted and disciplined by these drab ghosts. It is made up of them.

In the shady affair our deeper concern is this: such attraction as the master's while it should expand the tree and develop more of them is, instead, mortal enemy of the creative spirit that is the tree. It is by way of this mass-demoralization by imitation on a vast scale that we, as a nation, reached our present servility in the art of architecture and in its natural children the fine arts, with consequent dubiety in our way of life. The ugliness of all servile effort surrounds us as a kind of matter out of place in our man-made environment:

a kind of dishonor. Trees thus become fruitless; mountains become the plain; cascades the sea. All eminence becomes insignificant.

Yes, the substance may increase by such fatuous habituation as ours but man's faith dwindles as his inspiration grows dim or dies as his light goes out. So by way of irresponsible discipleship as by way of eclecticism of the styles, a native culture seems doomed to be stillborn. Meanwhile if a man, being unable to see into causes, must disqualify himself and dishonor an original by the imitation of effects—it is probably better for posterity that he emulate an admirable contemporary than an outlived style.

Neither custom nor habit of imitation exist in the world of the spirit. There, man's faith in himself—alone—has credit.

In that creative realm of ideas where all must be induced and nothing can be enforced, or taught, we find the great master—a living source. A flame. Centuries have come and passed with none. But there was never a period wherein prevailing distortion or downright perversion of the master's truth has not been occasioned by discipleship shallow as a mirror. Owing to a foolish, ignorant competition for technique before there is or can be any idea for which to use it, recourse to "the ready-made" takes the place of the self-sacrifice of interior discipline. The matter is not peculiar to us but is especially unbecoming and ungrateful.

It was the Buddha who noticed that the spoon may lie in the soup for a thousand years and never know the flavor of the soup.

Well . . . here I am giving you the great mother-art of architecture awaiting the return of her prodigal children—painting, sculpture, music—gone away five hundred years ago in search of a temple, each for itself. But "Christianity" is the prime example of how lovers of spirit have been betrayed by the desirous but unawakened disciple. Are we then, as a civilization, condemned to a graft upon a graft—for grafters?

INCAPABLE OF CONCEPTION THEY ARE MASTERS OF APPROPRIATION

I have heard those who were most indebted to the master deny him the loudest, and even those who would honor him most, distort, and so, torture his memory. Unawakened to conception as the gratuitous disciple seems to be by Nature, he is an ever-present detriment. And, where his human reactions as "artist" lie exposed for sale hidden under his own name, a cheat. He is the product of a foolish effort to put himself before his art— to put technique before developed sense. Even where, inspired by a creative mind like that of "lieber-meister," some of us have developed a mind of our own and honestly tried to live up to the clear beauty of truth according to the greatness to which we subscribed, these petty self-salesman appear to make imitations of effects by way of borrowed technique— that is to say, technique lifted or learned by rote, not by experience. Now, *each man's technique must be his own, his own way of getting his way with an idea.* But between the streamlining exploiter, the ignoramus, the canting critic, intelligentsia (men educated far beyond capacity) and this inflated peddler who calls himself an artist, we soon find even these undersellers of the ideas of others undersold by each other. Soon a smear of ready-made techniques erases all trace of spontaneous originality and our environment becomes a caricature of culture in the enlightened sight of men. Nor will any trace of the virtue— honor—of an original idea be found alive in the avoirdupois of our stupendous mass-education. By its capacious ministry insignificance becomes dear to the common herd and true significance disturbing to authority. The stupidity of academic authority, like the cupidity of the average merchant, serves only to confirm a tragic *lack of integrity* in our curiosity whenever we get out of the everyday rubbish heap to search for something superior. The true basis of every living culture will be found above and beyond this sham wherein both authority and education, for their own safety, are ever ready to combine against the inspiration of a man like Louis H. Sullivan. The net result to you and me is what? The waste of what might be the best of our lives. We, therefore, no longer have access to inspiration in this promiscuous prodigality of the vast commonplace; the massive mentality we presume to call "America" when we are but a small proportion of the Americas. Why not be modest and say USONIA? How quietly, almost imperceptibly, the great changes in Nature take place! How absolutely the great idealists who founded this country have disappeared from it except as memorials!

HONOR

The nature of a building material is its honor. The individuality of the man, his Nature and his stature, is his honor! No imitator knows honor. Supported by the brief authority which we call, with distrust, "government," our dishonor is our mobocracy. Its main support is imitation. Mobocracy swarms, and swamps what genuine democracy we have built into our commonplace, and our commonplace becomes a battlefield for divided interests.

No wonder we come to think upon innate honesty with pleasure and respectful reticence with delight.

No wonder Louis H. Sullivan died as he did. All great sayers and doers tire of the voluntary flattery of irresponsible disciples prematurely conspicuous, instead of finding joy in work kept alive by the faithful enthusiasm of devoted youth content to deepen to maturity by the interior discipline of voluntary sacrifice to an ideal. Sacrifice is no less necessary today than yesterday if there is to be a worthy tomorrow. There is no short-cut to the profound. The poignant Jesus himself was sick of discipleship with its taste for miracles. Would wisdom, then, dictate that the master be never generous but always wary? Well . . . it all lies beyond his control. His function is not to teach but to inspire. Instead of a "form follows function" scientist, I shall give you a great lyric poet.

DEEPER THAN THE TRUTHS OF PHILOSOPHER OR THE LAWS OF MORALITY IS THE SENSE OF HONOR

What is honor? Not the rules of a code—but the nature of honor. What would be the honor of a brick? That in the brick which made the brick a brick. What the honor of a board? Likewise—that in it that made the board a true board. Any material the same. Now mankind? A man's honor would be that which made the man true to himself as a man. What is his true self if not his individuality? Then what is the *quality* of his individual self but his honor? Now what would happen to him were he to imitate another? He would dishonor himself as himself. What would happen to the man he imitated? He would be diminished so far as could be, not expanded, and so be cheated. The imitator would steal twice: one theft from himself, the other theft from another. Often I have heard lieber-meister quote his paraphrase of Shakespeare's ' Who steals my purse steals trash,'—"Who steals my work steals my 'honor.' "

The more subtle and brilliant the disciple the sooner he will either mutilate the original form, while remaining unconcerned with the technique of the man who made it, or make a sorry mess of the master's technique while imitating "the look-of-the-thing," because where there is imitation there can be no understanding; that is to say, no love. There may be infatuation without honor.

In this continuous warfare of ambitions in which we live and are condemned to die a strange death in skepticism, a resentment or suspicion grows concerning success if other than money-success. Is such success felt as a reproach by the less successful? Consequently, a popular tendency results on the part of average people to patronize the imitator. He *is* nearer to them to be sure. A good enough practice were the imitator good, but bad because all imitation is bad. We have here another characteristic submoral pest—our provincial "patron-of-the-arts." Patronage, to be sure, but always at expense to someone else—probably to the master himself. Here we see a trait worthy of our mobocracy: wealth maintaining questionable imitations of genius as a kind of friendship or merchandise. Superior discrimination is not yet trustworthy enough for that foolhardy act and cannot be until the basis of good judgment has a better foundation than it can ever have on the basis of patronage, friendship, or "taste." The day is gone by when an artist could only be one if some prince or potentate sponsored him. In all great art in a free democracy *the nature of the thing is its honor* and art is its own patron.

But there are more damaging factors at work. To demoralize native cultural effort we have our kind of education. Schools everywhere encouraging the fool's race by rote for ready-made technique, a race for knowledge encouraged by the egotistic rationalizing of professors themselves near-failures as artists. But more especially, by the professed artist who in point of fact is but a routine scientist. As scientist he is no artist. So, why expect grapes from thorns?

THE FUNCTION OF EDUCATION IS TO TEACH MEN TO UNDERSTAND THEMSELVES

When men do understand themselves they may dedicate themselves to causes—they will never copy effects because then they will have their own, but by no short-cut. By becoming a self-evolving human being.

Unfortunately, if "educated" respectably no layman can *know* where the heart of the matter in architecture now lies unless he sees the work built and those living in it, for whom it was built. The whole matter of causes has been left out of his education. He lives wholly in effects. Nor can any routine scientist be able to teach him. Just as truth concerning the elusive depth-dimension involved in organic architecture defies the camera (being no cliché whatever), it will continue to elude the scientist and the intellectualist—the -gentsia. The great scientist may continue to furnish marvelous tools for the creative artist and the competent architect's tool-box but is himself impotent to make use of any one of them for humanity. Until architecture, philosophy, and religion become one as they are in organic architecture we are not going to be able to make such fruits of science as we already know in abundance, really constructive. We will remain disqualified by our own advantages. What hope then have we for indigenous *culture* when even our "universities" are not founded upon study of the principles and aesthetics of innate—or organic—structure and their architectural courses are therefore as wholly superficial as their own buildings would indicate, were all else adequate? Is art education itself a matter of ancient history because of the expediency to which we are committed on this battleground of divided interests, and are we therefore compelled to submit to ignorance of principle or equivocation wherever principles come into question? The affair has not changed much for the better these fifty-six years past since the master's time. We are living more than ever on the printed page. More and more our national life becomes vicarious. Is such mental distortion as ours, where reality is concerned, the inferior fruit peculiar to ever-present fear because we feel ourselves untrustworthy—a bad conscience being the price of our kind of "success"? Is there real necessity to make a dishonest success out of some division, subtraction, or multiplication of the so dubious means now afforded by our economic system? Is the so-called capitalist debt-system a fault to blame for this warfare of divided interests—where head and heart, soul and intellect, come in constant conflict and war is the necessary clearing house? Fear is the state of mind that gives the dictator power and war opportunity. Not physical but moral courage is the only trustworthy integral basis or ornament for an ethical democracy. Democracy is no faith for a moral coward.

But if an organic architecture is to grow it cannot subsist on effects, neglecting or hiding the causes of those effects in order to save the faces of pseudo-disciples. Whenever derivation is open and honest, eclecticism was its name in educational circles, and eclecticism still is the result of education itself. But even if discipleship were outright and honest, there is still neglect of a "cause" whenever the master is hung on the line "with the wash" at popular exhibitions. The quality of any original is so confused for the avid but ignorant public by odious comparisons so made by imitators with direct imitations, as to amount to a shameful or thankless exploitation of the original. The master is there but, to an ignorant public, he is already thrown in with outright backwash. Compelled to eat his own regurgitation he is with it on the way to obsolescence instead of on the way to the preservation of his quality as master. So the museum has become a morgue for the master and for the disciple a haven.

In all phases of our native cultural-endeavor the ingenuity we call "invention" is at a premium because we cannot now run our show or pursue our complicated existence without it. So by this substitution of prolix professionalism, prostitution of the "idea," and mere invention for creative art, we do get much of the dead-sea fruit—in the name of art— now so peculiar to our kind of life. In fact, mechanization is at bottom our fundamental "investment." So we are all one with the mechanics in a garage.

Whatever the cause of our "efficiency" may be or wherever remedy may lie, throughout our social fabric all forms of art-schooling or art-exposition have become unwholesome, infested by these agents of "effects." So everywhere we find the faithless disciple a handy "expedient" for "business"—a kind of growing of the fleece for the shears!

The habitual disintegration of the great value (a quality of the spirit) of any original is the inevitable consequence. How many trite or offensive things we are condemned to be and compelled to see because some venal verbalizer is deliberately confusing popular vision by playing down to fools until one might think the selling of some gadget or the clowning of a Picasso was our modern substitute for religion. By the very prevalence of constant super-emotionalized plugging for everything from a war hero to a cold cream by press, radio, and classroom, the visible environment in which we must live becomes—what it is: an insignificance at best—a shameful lie at worst. These establishments of our civilization, all too indicative of their insignificance, grow more dishonest day by day and stay that way.

Even now it is remarkable to me—as during all these past fifty-six years facing it on my own—to still see our so cocksure nation agreeably accept and proudly exhibit this plainly dishonest state of affairs, meantime calling this insignificance (which is its own tragic defeat where culture is concerned) *conservative!*

Any discipline when obsolete is a heresy.

Is heresy now conservative?

By way of the prefabricated disciple, the code-made and code-making expert, the synthetic professors of the so numerous "educated" neophytes with paper degrees in hand, or hoped for, architecture has become not a work of art at all but a technical makeshift: more than ever a mere piece of property. As for kindred "production," our big industrialists are so busily "streamlining" standardizations that we are not only compelled to see some egregious makeshift passed along as creation but also superficial effects instead of causes accepted as euthenics by the "higher education" and the officialdom it must please to live.

With the very temple thus profane what is our art? No more to us than the persistence of a desire to make the thing—whatever be the thing—seem like something not our own. Such creative sensitivity as we have, unless heroic, must soon be pervert to the sensational, the "monumental"—now a kind of "ham"; or the artist be induced by some businessman to "invent" something merchants can "sell" cheap to the credulous; or else the artist be destroyed. Artists themselves, most of whom are more ingenious than creative anyway, are willing to see invention as creation even when the "invention," though ingenious, is pernicious. Science, of course, receives the same sensations from the curious as from the beautiful. So does "invention." Lacking qualities of heart—therefore lacking the deep springs of true creation—neither science nor invention are now on good terms with art. Impelled by hope of profit or vicarious glory we see scientific invention released to our civilization and accepted by our institutions as a substitute for creative power. Who knows the difference? Therein, by help of the cheap services of the dishonest disciples of some creative mind, we have the present deluge of "box office": cheap old abuses maintained in new thousand-dollar gilt frames or old frames for new abuses, to "pack them in." "They" do not know when they are cheated or by whom. Is it by themselves? Of course, it is.

So, restlessly, we as a tirelessly exploited—and exploiting—people must find some release, if not refreshment, for whatever native love of beauty the god of creative impulse passed along to us by Nature. As the preceding generations found it in symbolism and the empty pretension called monumentality, so we find it in shoddy sensationalism, in new-fangled inventions or superficial beautifications by the commercial "designer" no higher than those of the professional beauty parlor or a cigarette in the fingers. "We" think we find—and we try to find—beauty in urbanism's streamlined machination; satisfaction in push-bottom power; entertainment in gadgetry, gag-ism; and happiness in preoccupation with so-called utilities of every kind that have no more spiritual significance than gangster-ism itself, a trip hammer or an all-day sucker in a baby's mouth.

At last—but not least—the line between the curious and the beautiful is become so confused by "modern architecture" itself that the dividing line between the curious and the beautiful which marks civilization itself from savagery or degeneracy—grows dim indeed. What recourse is there for the deeper more essential Usonian-self—(that self has a soul), should it be tempted to search for great repose: a serene and blessed mood? Say, peace. I refer not only to a political peace but to organic peace. Were we to find peace, a native culture true to democracy would be sure of some chance to emerge.

After all is said and done, I believe our missing native culture is due more to the lack of what constitutes a clear sense of honor than to any adverse material conditions. Youth is so soon old by ready-made techniques that any fresh inspiration of the ill-favored or even the unversed human interest is unlikely. Bewildered, the human being knows no true recreation, so no renewal, but must live, a surge of excitement in a splash of harsh, hot noise occasioned by the deluge of ingenious gadgetry to which our dated urbanism is now impelled to so completely surrender. But notwithstanding the desperate final recourse to "invention," see how many cherished (nevertheless impoverished) "inventors" are being washed up in the back yards of our world-challenging "successes"? Like our "artists" they are posthumously glorified, if glorified at all. Our favorite insult to our inventors as to our artists? These monuments we build to ourselves in their names! Throw in the statesmen.

Again—"*theories divorced from realities are bound to produce failures*"! But even our best people—our teachers ought to be our best—teaching premature techniques as though they were creative power itself, are unaware that the creative spirit and science are not even related except as an artist and his tool-box are related. Here in this ignorant—if innocent—assassination of spirit by science lies opportunity for the dishonest disciple, ruin to sincere apprenticeship, and the confusion of all true educationists where a native culture happens to be their real concern. Unless a miracle occurs, standard education today means eventual ruin to any true experiment which great art might try to make on its own account. Credit is gone. Science has destroyed it as it has religion. Perhaps this was no less so in times past in the older countries. But among us today, owing to so much greater opportunity and the vast spread of a lower level of promiscuous intelligence, any original impression that inspired art and architecture may make is like the print of a foot in the sand washed away by the next wave.

Of course, this sinister economic "system" (ours) in which without foundation we have at last so completely invested our future—and that of the world at Bretton Woods—*is* better served that way. Mobocracy *does* thrive thus and the economic unit, the buyer, is already so far conditioned in the direction of quantity instead of quality that the merchant's real profit lies in this oblique direction, and who in this attempted civilization (so tempted) is not a merchant?

The noble quality of a true original is so rare that its chief good is for the uses of these professional dealers in the infinite substitute—we call them our universities. But strangely enough—should "nature to her custom hold" and a true master appear among us today, as in the case of Louis H. Sullivan himself, he would first be suspect. Then he would be generally denied and ridiculed (but secretly envied) until his own individual creative force had been sufficiently diluted—that is to say, until the genius was plucked of the fruit of his ideas by disciples and the disciples, plucked by their disciples, had broken all down and divided it up among themselves until "the look-of-the-thing" became less strange and more easy for merchants of the ideas of others to propagate and "sell." Must the fount of original inspiration we call master be thus diminished or obscured? Yes. In a sense, a contemptible, unconfessed revenge for the kind of independent "success" a master himself is must—not in democracy but in mobocracy—take place. No one particularly to blame? The genius does not "belong." He will not "stay in line." In the place where guardianship of his inspiration should be found, there is only the artist himself. And the artist himself is a starveling.

The great master? Well . . . by now he is done. He is dead. Retribution to us for using him up, giving him away, or leaving him to die ignored is no longer likely. Nevertheless we are not through with him. Mobocratic "art" having a chronic bad conscience, if any, is more than ever likely to join the popular tendency to mob the tribe up by mobbing the master down. If the master has been much acclaimed, assassination by the tribe can be quite sure of mobocratic sympathy.

Admitting our society to be worse than tainted by this reverse (or abuse) of the democratic instinct, we are so far compromised concerning this social use of the genius and disrespect for his work, *as his own*, that not many of us (as we run in the pile) can "afford" to respect or would be able honestly to recognize our own origins. It is "bad taste" to even consider them, publicly. The truth is we only need keep silent, look as though we did it, and "the big wind" the master was is sure to go down in us. You see, we ourselves are becoming unable to recognize origins anyhow, even where feeble gratitude is moving us to do so. So why make such a foolish sacrifice? And even were we still able to recognize them why give ourselves away? For what? "We might have thought of it all ourselves anyway, but for 'him'."

Perhaps—as we are now set—there is no other means than grafting disciples to leaven, even a little, the inert lump of human ineptitude everywhere parasite upon art by way of this vanishing *ist* we call the art-*ist?* This creeping paralysis is chiefly in evidence in what we call "the higher learning."

Perfectly good fresh young lives—like perfectly good plums destined to be turned out perfectly good prunes.

Unenlightened "business," knowing it or not, freely patronizes this idea-deflation. Because it is cheap it is encouraged—and cheapens everybody. But how can we continue to call the deflation *conservative* and get away with it? By acting upon it (buying it), business actually cuts itself off from any radical progress in design beyond the petty gadgetry of the "streamlining" gentry, masters of "that new look" for *et cetera* and women. A radical architect sickens of the very word art if the professionalized streamliner, hired by the shrewd industrialist, gets "arty" to make more money for production by spitting on the apple and polishing it.

The master dead, sporadic attempts will be made to immortalize the poor man who died that the tribe might live. The memory of the great master should, by this time, be safely out of reach. But, as popular habit in Usonia is going, the master's "remains" are subject to disinterment and "debunking" to profit or please the swarms of those propagandists-for-the-literal, scribes of the pharisees—the Critics.

The literal will now be groomed to pass for the real; the shredded fact will become, by constant reiteration, preferred to the truth. Soon—who knows the difference between myth and truth? Now is the time when by getting out the brass band, making commemorative speeches, staging exhibitions, and throwing their hats in the air, they will only be making louder and bigger the mistake which neglect was in the first place. This demonstration will in itself only exaggerate betrayal and make celebration even more contemptible than neglect.

NOW HISTORY?

No matter how sincere the effort history may now be moved to make on behalf of the dead master, history is at best autopsy. Should the historian understand, interpret, or evaluate the mind of any great work individually inspired—the view is posterior for detractor and canonizer alike: the rump view! Inevitably these posterior views from the afterward are impressionistic distortion because naturally confined to rear-end perspective; or they are the personal slant of some personal sycophant or eru-edited partisan who doesn't know the difference—looking backward to see forward? As any critic is in his own nature, so in this supreme act of egotism—criticism—he not only now sees *as* himself but often sees as he does because he cannot see himself.

In the procession of posthumous academic "honors" that now proceeds, all will march together to a kind of popular entertainment or will help to maintain an expedient "museum" for mediocrity to be safely, if not infinitely, born into. Call this museum the university. Museums are what universities are becoming. These two have too much in common already.

Well, my confreres, if it moves us to compassion, anger, or pity to see what the multitudes of Usonian disciples settle for, a cheap synthetic that is themselves—how pitifully tragic it is to see what their patrons must settle for!

Education is far from the reality of education under the primitive conditions known as barbarism or even savagery. There at least the educator recognized the varying potentialities of the individual whether hunter, potter, weaver, or medicine man—and by actual experience his education proceeded.

Why do we try to make medicine men of hunters, potters, and weavers?

The artificiality of our mechanized society is helplessly drifting toward a bureaucracy so top-heavy that the bureaucracy of Soviet Russia will seem honest and innocent by comparison.

BOOK TWO   MIDDLE GROUND

CHAPTER ONE

THE ARTIST'S PERCEPTION SCIENCE LATER VERIFIES

Next to the science of profit-taking in our system and to science itself, the greatest current of mass production cherished in this union of states, which I am modestly calling Usonia, is education. "Education" is our heaviest investment in plant, money, personnel, and time. Looking at results, I would give you this as the main reason why our country is not yet on speaking terms with whatever there might still be living of its own organic culture. Popular education is served by patterns preaccepted by authority as most certainly *respectable*. Preferably dead. Anything alive is dangerous. "Respectable" patterns, in the ceaseless turmoil of such vast mobocracy as ours, have become the prefixed patterns of either provincial-Colonial, *papier-maché* French, Oxfordian or pansy Greek, German Bauhaus, or the stencilized cliché for sterility now called "modern," though modified Italian or even German Baroque might do. There are so many other names to fill in with or (literally) fall back upon! Or, because our universities, judging by the damage they do to truth and beauty by their prefabricated "respectability"—such as the buildings they build for themselves—education has neither independent will nor the least taste for the affirmation that is *inception*. Should we say, then, that our universities are being served as education *must* be served in order to keep on being our leading standardized industry? Above the cherished processes of standardized mimicry which I have described, what else can be done by such overgrown knowledge-factories as we continue to propagate at this time, swollen by millions of the boys from our villages and farms and now over-flowing with the G. I.? Wholesale barter of freedom for intellectual slavery is what we are calling "the higher education." See in it, all but a little corner, the complete capitalization of our fears and deepest prejudices. We are continually mistaking both for our holiest feelings. By ministration of the "higher education" our mentality lives on the quote and manages to be as easily scared by originality as it is easily pleased to defend standard insignificance.

Instead of the good old advertising slogan we used to see along the American roadsides, "Quality knows no substitute"—let's present regents of the "higher education" A.D. 1948 with this one: "Give us quality, O genius, because we—swearing by the armchairs of the select in behalf of future armchairs—can make quality good for any quantity of substitutes." Yes ... our greatest national industry thrives on the substitute for all other substitutions: the great god expedient. "They" are in the habit of calling this—their god—the practical!

Meantime the manners and morals of higher education are expedient. Its regents are expedient. See the pestiferous scholastic locutions of Oxford-Gothic they plan, plant, and cultivate ad libitum ad museum! They are all too, too expedient! Cast-iron Gothic or symbolic Traditional. Cape Cod Colonial, L'Enfant Classic, or Jeffersonian-homesick—the flat-bosomed, wide-bottomed stencil (the box on stilts)—or the international quilt: any one of them will show how it all works, and what really is the difference between them?

Schooling once so "fixed," great issues dwindle in this nation or stew in our own bigotry. By way of the servility of the imported university professor or the native factory-made school our once great and original hope for a democracy seems doomed. The struggle for power by immoral international power-politics, conscription, bureaucratic proscription, fraudulent "service," and flat-minded "brass," all of which have come up from behind to overtake us and be democracy's well-meaning, if not holy, executioners.

Yes ... great master, with patiently moderated invective I cite here what I have heard, immoderate, from your own lips. You a lyric poet born too soon, frustrated, starved back to the back room in a cheap hotel in an urban rubbish heap at a time when our cultural establishments were heedlessly, as needlessly—even greedily, servile to mass money-power, perpetuating by easy billions the materialism that grips us now! Materialism so dense that even then the consequences of originality were like those of criminality! So this new democratic architecture we call organic and is original may again be swamped by the same heedless mobocracy or more likely by official statism (the two gangsterisms do work together) and our hope of organic culture will be left to die with principle in this Western wasteland! But more dangerous to any quiet hope for our cause is the congenital copying of superficial effects and persistent neglect of fundamental causes. Yes ... all down the line!

But, dear master, you know it to be in the nature of the ideas of great men and their causes to "die" only to be born again! Ignorant of its own destructive character where human nature is our real concern, the enormous money-power we derived from exploiting a new land by the great "industrial revolution" is power on the wane. Illusion! Its doom is its own assembly line! The chemical revolution is here to make even that vast matter of power powerless. The more amazing its establishments the sooner obsolete.

Born of the industrial revolution comes, now, another—the chemical revolution. Again a demand that our architecture dig deeper and broaden anew. But the old moral, economic, political pretensions (they were never essence truly humanized) were already failing. They were dated and going before the A-bomb appeared to mock them, mock this external type of building we inherited from a dead past and erect by the mile in facades like Radio City. Now the city is within a city. An internal turnover deliberately ingrown to intensify the folly of centralization so far as humanity is concerned. Another crucifixion! This time by the private richman. Re-crucifixion of the general crucifixion by patronage of vast, conscienceless machine-power.

If in the light of this latest involution our present state of civilization is going to prove more fit for human life here on earth than barbarism, we are where decentralization is, more than ever, democracy's right challenge to the old order! That challenge is now made one with democratic ideology itself. Democracy, to survive, must mimic no more! Certainly not mimic its own past! Mimicry is not emulation. Sentimentality is not sense.

Traditions? Yes, beloved master! Scores of them will die in order that major Tradition have a chance to live! Codes? Yes, they too are stubborn impediments to great work but were they true abstractions—patterns of truth—they might be truly useful. Because they are not essential, but mostly the routine habit of mind of small-minded experts for fools, codes will die or drastic revisions be made in them by Nature herself. In our multitudes of ready-made or canned techniques, why not try to make the code at least honest? Do not try to make it "foolproof." A "foolproof" code would always be murder of the future by fools for fools. Even though yet unable to make codes true democratic abstractions—that is to say, flexible enough to stand as genuine "essence"—at least provide for timely appeal! Not as architects nor as men can we fail to possess the individual courage necessary to face the divided interests of the baudy "balance of trade." We cannot do this manly spadework short of wholehearted affirmation of the same principles put to work on codes and their framers that are now characterizing our vision of an organic architecture. *The new reality?* Yes, citizen. If we want to really live in fruitful peace instead of frightful conflict, the simple principles of organic architecture not only contain the basis but are the center line of any possible establishment of a form for a true democratic order.

Instead of allowing education to condone or promote more confusion by glorified propaganda—trying to enforce any symbolic abstraction whatever, however sacred (even the dollar sign), let us allow no more heartless mechanical techniques to pass for human artistry on the strength of any authority however "high," remembering the law is always stretched in favor of the official against the citizen.

CHAPTER TWO

ARE WE AS WE SEE?

Sitting alone so far away from the master, yet so near, for a page or two just for the view, come along with me beyond that now ancient incident (fifty-nine years ago) to speculate somewhat upon the why and wherefore of heretic seeking heretic by instinct amounting to intelligent choice. Why did the older novice and the neophyte not only find each other but find themselves congenial from that first moment?

Well . . . I have always regarded "birth" as inevitable invocation (blood lines tracing far back beyond slumbering instinct or living memory). So to go into this seemingly haphazard vis-à-vis might not only be amusing but informative?

In mind, this question: is there always something of archaic impulse still alive in us to reshape the ever-present confusion disconcerting our immediate present? As have men themselves, so have their architectural forms, once individual and noble at the beginning, grown weaker and weaker instead of stronger and stronger owing to strictures of geometric time? This complex limitation we call "age" seems to have come along to make materialism the more inexorable. Is our mathematics a mental device to so fix upon the human mind its "one, two, three" dimensions as to construct a prison house of and for that mind: a finality devised regardless of the benign nature of the human soul?

Sometimes I wonder if "time" was devised only to make this "one, two, three" life that scientists will themselves someday know so much more about, a life not of childlike limitations but one of childish imitation? Was time, as we now account it, designed for the shopkeeper and the counting house, eventuating in machinery, standardizing, and "age"; or were shopkeeper, counting house, machinery, and age designed for time?

Length! Breadth! Thickness! Three dimensions only? For the creative individual they are not enough. At least we must expand the third to a fourth capable of integral concepts like "form and function are one" in order to encounter the feeling for principle in this imminent search of the innate self for selfhood. Manhood not selfish. The feeling for principle was the valid source then, is now and hereafter the true source of creative sensibility.

What I am trying to say amounts to something like this: life itself is a splendid unfolding—a coherent plasticity: so there can be no real *beginning* in this or any mortal conjunction on this earth. Nor—according to the principle of organic change as we may sense it in organic architecture—end to be foreseen. Master and worshipful workman are sitting together at this moment still of and yet amid countless unperfected or perverted lives in this ever vital continuous affair of environment.

The perversions of great ideas, if not all hope, surround these two. To confound them? No, to *condemn* them! Because this moment is (the present always seems to be) a most degenerate moment when all truth is dangerously radical. Yes, this is a moment far down if not the lowest moment in the twentieth-century poetry-crushing era in which Usonians live. Life is again deformed by a more violent divorce from nature than ever before. This time the divorce is had by way of licentious abuse of new power; machines. Humane life is so used in consequence that whatever existed for man above the belt he stupidly betrays by lack of integrity in the curiosity of his "intellect" and the cupidity of his instincts. He is calling this curiosity science, and his cupidity—business. His reward is—at bottom— ugly waste misnamed progress. Sanitation and hygiene of the body it is, but soul slaughter such as no god-of-things-as-really-made ever looked down upon among the children swarming on this infested, ravished earth. Earth, "where every prospect pleases and only man is vile."

GLANCE AT THE SCENE

Unspoiled Usonian landscape is already drawn and quartered, literally, by the old-time surveyors putting immediate convenience above future benefits. We inherit the land from them piecemeal in rectilinear "pieces," regardless of topography. The pieces are called plots. Division lines, great and small, run due North to South and East to West, dooming every structure (placed parallel to them) to one hot and bright side and one cold and black side. Natural features of our fresh beautiful Usonian landscape are thus, at the beginning, crucified by commonplace efficiency.

Notwithstanding limitless, available space in our vast new domain where population is only beginning, every single building in town (dwelling or otherwise) toes the street line—close up, according to old London town. Coal is fuel here as there, so all houses huddle straight up and stick tight. The monarch passed on the street, so—eyes front! Buildings in Chicago, as in London, were there and then adapted to "His Highness." Now, his highness is the "passer-by." Coach and horse or the Foot and Walker line, perhaps the horse-car or a hansom cab came along the London street. So all this over here took place as was the ancient habit "over there." Habit was again shamelessly taking root where it could never belong if men were men with faith instead of nostalgia.

Should more freedom be wanted by some man—impractical, intractable dweller ("Why ever would the man want it?"), more space if and when found was put into a bigger front-yard on the street!—dedicated yes, as always, to the "passer-by"—now his lordship. Few town or country residents ever thought or even dreamed of individual privacy as charm. Except as it was a slum affair (rectal or concerned with the upper region of the pantaloons), privacy was no moving concern.

The resultant pattern of an "American" village, subsequently of our cities (they are all only over grown villages), became the familiar one of a pair of scissors or the cast-iron criss-cross of dressy, military rank-and-file: eyes always front; "fronts" always obediently facing their commanding officer—the "passer-by." The "front porch" was our local improvement of the imported features of our domesticity. (We invented pie, porches, and ice water.) For the underdog, as monarchic hangover, came along the twenty-five-foot "lot." Hangdog fate for the lesser man stalling him in ranks and stanchions by the mile. Party walls in the circumstances became the brutal raw-brick masses we now see everywhere glooming against the sky, cutting human habitation to pieces: indiscriminate crucifixion of the criss-cross itself.

Bedeck this whole prisoned, regulated, but inchoate hash of fresh opportunity with loud-screaming signs—come-on-in signs everywhere urging competition, the bigger and noisier the "sign" the better—and what have you? You have what we had then to work in, work with, and work upon. In it all not one attempt at a thought-built building. No one had ever seen one!

Dwellings, high and low, each in all and all in all, were trying hard to be different from each other, each craving distinction; and by trying so hard to be "different" all succeeded in being only the same in a general fiasco. All are bastardized echoes of bad old King George's court; or, if preferred, take a little Italianate palazzo in scagliola, caricaturing in Chicago the aristocrats of the now futile monarchic era of the Italian magnificent, Lorenzo. But from George came the pseudo-manor's wooden posts, imitating marble columns under classic wooden pedimentia, while we fought so hard to be free from him and all his courtiers represented. Queen Anne fronts were for Mary Ann behinds fashionable at this time. The fallacious "front" was all that mattered anyway. The "dickie" or false shirt-bosom, the celluloid detachable collar and cuffs went along with the ornate facade, or "front." Have you seen—from behind—the "fronts" worn in the parlors by the women of that period to match the architecture?

The women beckon. Step within and see the fussified boxes they inhabit: boxes stacked or pushed together by climbing or descending stairs—boxes partitioned off into little boxies, boxlets, or boxettes—pigeonholes for every domestic function imaginable: water-tight and nearly airtight. Yes—and soon you will see every domestic function fitted for and into only some box. Great mansions? Yes—plenty of them. But they were only bigger, more extravagant boxing. The box better brushed and stuffed—that's all. The more ornate everything was, the better. It took a heavy dose to move that era to aesthetic emotion! Outsides were freely, most expensively bedeviled by the gift of ignorance called taste. Do you know why the word taste? The small windowed box even then belonged to a bygone age when glass was taxed and modern heating was nonexistent.

The wood-butcher's cut-and-butt carpentry was everywhere seen stiffly sticking up over "rock-face" masonry, all according to the elect—and alert—"classic" designers of that lost period. This "classic" went to the plasterers for any tune they might care to play with a trowel on its insides. The witchery of the interior decorator (inferior desecrator) ran away in every direction to dress and overstuff the whole thing: ultra-insides for ultra-outsides. In really fashionable circles, all materials for furnishing, good or bad, went into the hands of the "draper" and their nature either died there of ruthless rape or committed suicide in shame. The murdered woodwork had already met an especially savage death by turning lathe, shaper, or jigsaw. What craftsmen were left—they were destroyers of good material—were even then limiting apprenticeship and—knowingly or not—turning them-selves as well as their "unions" over to the assembly line. This wholesale crucifixion of human nature on the outside was habitually shunted to the "inside"-architect for beau-tification. It was the inside-architect who presided over the "stuffings" and crowded the hangings. The result resembled an overdressed woman of the period half dressed for a party. The inside-architect never once thought to venture outside the inside, nor the outside-architect inside the outside. I used to wonder why not? Was it because woman's place was in the "home" and so the inside was usually left to the "taste" of some neces-sitous or ambitious "society" woman?

So far as buildings then went, or now go on the restless realtors' merciless rounds, the "lousy bastard" (even then the realtor's pet name) was always there first. The *"mise en scène"* not only made no sense but had no mercy on the desired eye and was proud of it. Total abortion by way of purposefully deformed materials in artful effort to make them appear like some other material—the first rule of the game—ruled out both sense and aesthetic sensibility. Honest? No matter! Dishonesty was more "artistic"! Is yet. Gables, dormers, minarets, bays, porches, oodles of jiggered woodwork ruthlessly painted, poking in or peeking out of piles of fancified stonework and both playing idiotic tricks with each other, just to captivate that desired eye? Oh, no: just to inflate some well-to-do owner's sense of himself—the owneress as she saw "himself." Believe me, physical torture was merciful to man in comparison with this irrepressible, badly managed desire to evacuate illicit excrescence. The prevailing motive seemed to be not only to kill by way of terrible "taste" the simple nature of man but to kill everything that touched him—especially whatever materials he touched—by making them all belie or belittle themselves, and do a caricature of the property-instinct for posterity. "Himself" seemed to want, desperately, to become somebody or something else. Man, the executioner, now not only killed to eat and killed for sport—he killed for culture.

No wonder I prayed—then—for negation!

Big or little houses, schools, banks, stores, churches—even privies—were thus badly, even madly, excrescent. All life connected with this excited bedevilment was utterly bedizened. The pernicious social fabric so excruciated by adornment was a moral, social aesthetic excrement that was only the rubbish heap of a nation-wide waste of all natural resources. As for sensitive aesthetics, the whole town from any sane point of view was obscene of everybody in it and all truths of being except one: vulgarity. *Even that had a bad time being honest!* Public buildings were only worse. They exaggerated the demand for this uxorious shamelessness and raised it to the nth degree. A kind of outrageous grandomania prevailed wherever money could be found or debt incurred. But these showpieces of sham were only the canned relics of monarchic grandeur; the "classic" the very best people still called for. But even at best it was callow, or canned, ornamentia. The authors of this downright dementia kept clear of the insane asylum only by the foolish pride of their clients in collecting the fifty-seven varieties of banal sentimentality that could, even then, be bought ready-made. Especially the wisdom of the "shrewd" became idiotic when they dared "show off" their idea of ornamentalitis. Even the worthy could not resist this orgy of the ornate.

Stupid? No. Just wicked *extravagance* passing for luxury—advertising to posterity that its owners were not on speaking terms with either scholars or gentlemen.

To begin the town and end it like a boy hankering for the circus there was actually a preference by the best people for contortion. This act on the flying trapeze seemed to entail that recklessness which marked this period of magnificence and expense. Chicago loved it and maintained it in the name of a "good society," mainly the prostitute relic of King George's court. And how did the patterns of this flotsam and jetsam get to "George" in the first place? To him from "Louie" in Paris, of course! Where to Louie from Paris? Probably from the Italian, "Lorenzo." In any case, all that was hallowed in English landscape or tasteful in the Renaissance itself was completely left out. Here where bountiful opportunity existed for dignified indigenous culture in freedom of space and beauty of materials, the avid license of a foolish, hungry orphan turned loose in a bakeshop was mistaken by riches for freedom!

Throughout this rebirth of so many rebirths of the Renaissance no item of horrendous misuse of wealth had ever been dignified by Nature's innate significance. *Nature was just "outdoors"!* Inner significance of architecture had been lost to symbolism some five hundred years before. Yes, and here now at home, with a new people in a new land for a fresh start, was this defamation of native character by riotous excess in the name of respectability— and respectability meant the bastardy of any and every outlived European style. Defiant of good sense or repose, here came "taste" with the Pig and the Poet on either side of the Chicago tripartite shield—both rampant! Outrageous license had found the machine and the machine had quickly won it over to its side. Again democratic freedom went under to mobocratic license. The ulterior mission of machinery now seemed to be to make the baudy showy; to crucify even vulgarity itself on its own terms—to see it squirm and hear it scream. So good machines in the hands of sudden wealth ground, tore, and bound. Or rode the lives they might have served to save but for their prostitution to this ignorant showmanship of too easy, irresponsible ownership. The great unmoral power of the modern industrial revolution had come to give meum and tuum all they could take for the grand gesture and waste the rest—to keep prices high, if for no other reason! Gigantic leverage was here in childish men's hands before even good men were qualified to use it to human advantage. Here came the newly discovered short-cuts to promiscuous power that gave the grand short-circuit to (and for) modern culture and landed us right where we are: "the only great nation to have proceeded directly from barbarism to degeneracy with no culture of our own in between."

To further crucify this gladsome celebration of wealth accelerating the grand cruci-fixion by machinery, came now our ever-present "modern advantages": corporate machines set up in palatial offices by vested interests (bankers), sitting behind massive Corinthian columns to control the masses of machinery. "*Public-service*" corporations were already entering upon the fresh landscape with meters, poles, and wires instead of bayonets and guns. Wherever people "settled" came these new strictures of the "investment" to devas-tate the future in the name of taxed human convenience. Poles and wires came to be to the investment that was the human being what the wire fence was to the investment that was cattle. Stark poles were bestrung with miles on miles of endless wiring. They marched alongside the streets to be looked through or to look by or look at. In towns a devastating forest, in the country a searing slash at the eye that would look upon whatever there was left to contemplate of beauty of Nature that had been let alone. Now came these corporate "follow-ups" of the tin can and barbed wire that had "conquered" and bound the waste-lands of the west, hand and foot. Poles and wires in that pioneer day became the irredeem-able mortgage on our landscape which they still are *a century later!* The entire "*mise en scène*" was being ruthlessly ravished by "power." The modern Goliath was on the job. The measured tread of the Golem was heard in the streets. Voracity had become speed. By grace of "public service," here came ruthless crucifixion of all the crucifixions gone before.

The already habituate internal-combustion engine is running away with any co-ordinate humane planning the scene was ever going to know: these antique spacings of the village which now made the entire arrangement of the town are becoming dangerous and a farce in the cities. Excess gadgetry, too, is beginning to sneak or leak into the old order which was stranger to them than they were to it. There in the buildings of the old "classic ' dispensation now a heresy, the gadgets were like so many shiny new brass buttons on some old derby hat. In truth, the derby hat, kimono, and gaiters were harmonious compared to this violent revel of infelicity. Barbarous? No. Not so good! Man's abode on earth *dehumanized* in the name of an idealized but already licentious motive for a civilization? Profit. A game? Ah, yes . . . that was it! Nothing we had to live by or could now live with or live for had such simple integrity as barbarism, although this was a kind of pseudo-barbarism itself. The main feature of human associations today is that the vast majority prefer strife to fearless frankness. Is that degeneracy? Why then look back and call this a civilization? Let us look forward beyond glorified hypocrisy.

CHAPTER THREE

THE GLIMMER AND THE COURAGE

Our human aesthetic sensibility? Well—as we all know now—the cutworm forgave the plow! "They" all, or nearly all, forgave the corp that crucified them and bought stock in the enterprise that nailed them together with their own democracy upon the criss-cross. This plain cupidity and the stupid curiosity called scientific were both looked upon as *progress!* The swift march of the machine was no longer stealthy but pageantry in the streets. Disorder, dissonance, and discord composed this stunning symphony for the necessitous convenience of the human animal. Do men rise above such degradation of themselves, by themselves, by their own effort? If they do, it must be because of the slender thread of light—this glimmer or gleam of sensibility sure to be left somewhere to cheer the man: the sweating, straining artifex.

The immortal future of mortal humankind not only now depends upon that immemorial glimmer which we must call the sensitivity of the creative artist but upon his courage. Our peace as a whole people lies there too, in need of courage—in that same light. No science can substitute for Nature without foreign wars as a clearing house.

A nation industrialized beyond proper balance with its own agronomy is a menace to its own peace and the peace of the world. It is a house in a chronic state of civil war always divided against itself.

BOOK THREE   FOREGROUND

CHAPTER ONE

THE STRUCTURE OF THE FIRM

To go back to the "glimmer and the gleam"—the master sitting there so immediate; absorbed in a pattern for integral ornament before him on his drawing board: he was untroubled by any of this. He took it in his stride. I could never see that "lieber-meister" had more or less than a creative conscience. He was born Bostonian but primarily of a Spanish dancer and an Irish dancing master. Sensitivity to beauty was thus in his immediate background although Boston was his foreground. As luck would have it he inherited money enough to enable him to go about as he pleased. Time came he went to the Beaux Arts in Paris where the young urbanite might become a sophisticate Parisite. Neither knowledge of nor any desire for the warm simple ways of country life were ever seen in him. He accepted the economic situation as he found it. I never heard him mention "the machine."

But I, the designing partner's "pencil" flung there beside him, inherited a troublesome Puritan strain. I was Bostonian too, but only in passing. Taken to that hallowed vicinity at the age of three by a music-loving lawyer-doctor-preacher-father I lived in a Weymouth parsonage from the age of three to the age of eleven: there to be kindergartened (the Froebel way) by my unitarian teacher-mother. She wanted an architect for a son. It is perhaps significant that golden curls beloved by mother were down on my shoulders until, when eleven, I was sent to work on the farm. Aged six I had been sent to Miss Williams's hand-picked private school, devoted, I guess, to bringing up little Lord Fauntleroys. But returning West eventually to enter Wisconsin's university, I—aged eleven—was sent to work spring and summer with my unitarian farmer-uncles in their "valley," near Spring Green, there by the beautiful sand-barred Wisconsin River. These Welsh relatives of mine were called "free thinkers." They were Unitarians. Up to and including this time, when I have looked over at ourselves and tried to glimpse fate, I was usually having difficulty raising carfare. My father was intellectual preacher-musician at this time so, and therefore, indigent. But mother's people were fairly prosperous yeomen, gladly supplying any missing sustenance for this roving, Sanskrit-writing, music-loving parent's family. Owing to my mother's prenatal wish I had, all my life long, looked forward to being (at first to me because of my mother) that sacred-hero: the architect! Dissatisfied with college training there, where architecture was not; impatient by nature, I had said goodbye to Dean Conover, a few callow fellow-"engineers" and walked out of Wisconsin U. Three months more and "they" would have given me a degree as civil engineer. I have had the same contempt for "degrees" ever since.

The designing partner left Paris disgusted with the grandiloquent Beaux Arts "projects" which, by this time, he seemed to have shed completely. But while in Paris, besides the standard vices of the "immortal city" (those tragic ones that eventually cut him down before his time), he had met John Edelman. I believe John was the first real educational influence Louis H. Sullivan ever found. And John was Bostonian too. John from now on was quoted to me. Often. The master-to-be had evidently fallen under "John's" influence and seemed to share many sentiments which "John" habitually expressed, and expressed with forcible profanity. Both despised Boston for some reason. And so, for some reason, I thought I did.

Nor had I any brief for my own education at the University of Wisconsin except outside work afternoons in the private offices of the dean of the engineering department, Allan D. Conover. The kind-hearted dean generously paid me a then no mean stipend of thirty dollars each month. But now, I, the unwilling "engineer," country-loving heretic (but no rustic), was in under a far more sophisticated heretic. If in me Louis H. Sullivan had found a serviceable pencil in his hand for better or for worse, I had found in him the ideal iconoclast. Nevertheless, in my credulous adoring breast was disquieting disapproval of the private ways of the master-to-be.

Although he did seem untroubled by a social conscience, he but seldom swore and in money matters was immaculate. Seeing only moral no ethical quality in either, I was heedless in both, believing punctilio with money tied up with meanness; "Were they trying to make the damned thing sacred so they could keep on playing their game safely?" Well ... I've learned a lot about "money" since. I regarded swearing as I was taught: as unbecoming—ugly, a bad noise, repulsive like a bad smell; ventilation really. I despised smoking, then, drinking, whoring, and do now. I despised *the habitual in any form.* And

L. H. S. practiced them in their many forms to a dreadful extreme. Poison himself to lose his real self just for what? Why go around following a filthy incendiary sticking out of his face? Just to give an imitation of something on fire inside? I guess the cigarette is something of a relief to paws disengaged when the human animal rose upon its feet. But the animal in me wanted and expected more from him than just that! Ah—arrogance! Of course, and—I see it now—I was a disagreeable character too.

I know the popular reaction to this confession, but I make it on no moral grounds whatsoever. Nor do I make it with a sense of superiority. Am I making it as evidence of my good luck?

By Louis H. Sullivan's side in those now faraway days, he thirty-four, "Wright" the young draughtsmen nineteen, he would often say to me with undisguised contempt: "Wright! I have no respect at all for a draughtsman!" Certainly he so conducted himself toward them but, as the other draughtsmen quickly noted, never so toward me. His haughty disregard had already offended most of the Adler and Sullivan employees. Embarrassing episodes were frequent. His contempt may have been due to the fact that he was so marvelous a draughtsman himself. But I knew what he really meant.

In the offices on the top floor of the old Borden block, "Wright!" "Wright!" rang out over the draughting room whenever he needed me, which was pretty often. With no hesitation whatever, "Wright" came whenever "Mr. Sullivan" called. Only long years after I had left the Adler and Sullivan office did he ever call me "Frank."

He taught me nothing nor did he ever pretend to do so except as he was himself the thing he did and as I could see it for myself. He ("the designing partner") was the educational document in evidence. I learned to read him with certainty just as you shall see him and see me if you are a good reader between the lines. I am sure he would prefer it—that way.

THE PENCIL IN HIS HAND

Regularly Saturday night, this now regular (but markedly favored) employee of Adler and Sullivan would pick up at the outer office an envelope with sixty dollars in gold pieces, minus the stipend to pay off for the funny little house ("they" used to ask me if it were Seaside or Colonial) which a subsequent contract with the "firm" had enabled me to build in Oak Park. The sum was high wage in those more innocent (or less exploited) days: about two hundred and fifty dollars now? I would take the firm's gold with me to "saints' rest," as the self-righteous, fast-growing suburb "Oak Park" was nicknamed. I was still twenty-one, with a wife seventeen, when a son was born. In my name, altogether too fast, a premature little family began to grow up in that "funny little house." In exchange for the firm's gold advanced to build the house, without reading it I signed a lawyer's five-year contract with the "firm of Adler and Sullivan." This contract after working in their office for nearly two years.

To see Mr. Sullivan (the designing partner) you must know him not only by the pencil in his hand that was me, but you must also know Dankmar Adler, the senior partner! "The big chief" we called him. And, too, you must remember the way firms practicing architecture were made up about fifty-five years ago. They are still made that way. First, there was the manifest *success*, outstanding member of the concern, senior partner. Next came the "designing partner"—he in the back room behind the scenes—who, at least, must know how to draw well and (turn out plans, maybe) certainly make the *pictures*. And often there was the front or "contact" man—a "mixer"; probably a well-heeled socialite. The mixer it was who brought in the "jobs" and kept the firm in the club window for sale.

In order to "get the job" (the first principle of architecture as laid down by great-big H. H. Richardson), this more decorative "intermediate," Dankmar Adler never seemed to need. The big chief was so well provided with "jobs." But he did need the designing partner—desperately—for the great engineer-constructor had graduated into architecture from the army. The designing partner had appeared at the moment when Adler's prowess and practice as an architect were both established and rapidly growing. Many important Chicago clients, merchants like Alexander Revell, manufacturers like Martin Ryerson, wholesale merchandisers like Selz-Schwab, theatre magnates like Horace McVicker, and big industrialists like Andrew Carnegie were his clients. Several rabbis (and numerous wealthy Jewish clients, all of whom would have only Adler) came to sit waiting in his outer office. Also Adler's personal influence in the ranks of the A. I. A., at that time an honorable body of proven practitioners, was immense. Dankmar Adler was a solid block of manhood, inspiring the confidence of everyone, a terror to any recalcitrant or shifty contractor. His ideas throughout were advanced far beyond his time, as his choice of a partner would indicate, and he was known even in those more liberal days (before architecture became obsessed by college degrees) as a liberal, original thinker. Reading (or rereading) some of the papers he prepared and read to the A. I. A. at that time, for instance, the paper, "Modifying Buildings by the Use of Steel," would astonish most modernites.

One day there came to this liberal strongman in the profession still a noble one, a not so tall young man with a stride seeming quite too long for the length of his legs. The net result of the stride was a pompous strut. Carrying a dark pointed beard well out in front of a dark-brown head of hair trimmed fairly short, already "losing" at the crown, he came immaculately—as always—dressed in brown. His eyes were large, also brown; burning, "seeing" eyes that had a glint of humor in them to make the arrogance of his bearing— bearable. He had offered himself to the big chief because—well, the Bostonian novice hadn't been too successful since he returned from marking time in bad company at the Paris Beaux Arts for a term of about two years. John Edelman, his mentor there and friend now in this country, had announced Adler to him and (I suspect) him to Adler. Sullivanian virtuosity at the time was entirely that of the amateur draughtsman-designer.* But in that respect he had won Adler's instant recognition as virtuoso and the young Spanish-Irishman from Boston (yes, and Paris too) was installed in the Adler back room. The long-

* See early designs made at the Beaux Arts.

coveted and now welcome "designer" had arrived. Adler never lost faith in that growing phase of Sullivan's genius nor ever failed him but once. Of that? More later.

Anyway, the grand chief knew enough building construction for two or more. And the Sullivan schooling in practical planning of buildings actually built began then and there under ideal auspices: ideal because the chief was not only an experienced engineer but was also a splendid planner himself; a good critic, as his choice of a "designer" was to prove. He was one of the few farsighted men in the free-for-all catch-as-catch-can "classic" of these late nineties. But the grand chief was never classic. He was independent. Inexorably honorable, he possessed an architect's practice already so well established in his favor that his clientele resented the young Irishman. "Adler was good enough for them." Some few left the chief on account of Sullivan. But soon curiosity became appreciation and designs proceeding from the young sophisticate in the back room began to please not only Adler but Adler's captious clients. Chicago, a city rapidly rising to greatness, down there on the prairie—or in the swamp where the wild onions grew that gave the city its Indian name—was already a gigantic railroad center, a vast stockyards serving the entire U. S. A. Big crude Chicago—destined to become the most beautiful American city! A few years later Chicago began to take notice not only of Adler but to exhibit a friendly curiosity concerning his new "designer."

Prompted by Ferdinand Peck, when the matter came up, Adler was naturally the man to be entrusted with a great civic enterprise like the Chicago Auditorium to seat five thousand people. So the "big job" was given to Adler for good reasons. He had built the Exposition Buildings on the lake front, Central Music Hall on Randolph and State Streets, and many commercial buildings beside the several Chicago theatres. All have now disappeared. The five million dollars that great building was to cost then would be about ten or fifteen million now. After several years on comparative "chicken feed" (store and loft buildings because the firm steadfastly refused to build residences), Louis H. Sullivan came into this important commission by way of Dankmar Adler's prowess in his chosen profession.

At this great moment in his own life as well as in the life of the "firm" the designing partner was looking for someone to help him with the "Auditorium" drawings. The great building project was casually called "The Auditorium."

I appeared before Mr. Sullivan soon after my initial year in Chicago with residence architect J. L. Silsbee: Silsbee—rising star in the residential work of that day. A fellow draughtsman working at Syracuse aristocrat Silsbee's office, by name Wilcox (he was one of five minister's sons working for Silsbee at the time—Silsbee himself was a minister's son), said he had bragged of me a little to Mr. Sullivan. Wilcox had himself tried for the job but failing to qualify he asked me to respond to an invitation to come to see him which he carried to me from Mr. Sullivan. I went. Mr. Sullivan seemed to like me but tossed aside the drawings (manifestly made under Silsbee's influence) which I had with me.

"No! No!" said he. "Silsbee draws well but draw something of *your own* and bring it to me after I get back from the A. I. A. conference in St. Louis."

Congenital, and now congenial heretic (I liked so much the knowing way he looked me through and through), I wanted to work for him above all others because already the firm of Adler and Sullivan was known as revolutionary even in the architecture of that unconsciously—but naturally, thank God!—revolutionary time. So with great excitement I worked in my room at the Watermans' (where I was lodging) and brought a dozen or more drawings to show him. He glanced at them, studied a few intently for a moment, and said:

"Wright, you have a good touch . . . and you'll do. How much do you want?"

Doubling on what I was getting from Silsbee, I told him, surprising him by the moderation of the demand.

"All right," said the incipient master indulgently, "we can fix that up as you go along." And the relationship began that was to last about seven years. Designing partner thirty-four. "Pencil" nearly twenty.

In Dankmar Adler, Louis H. Sullivan had a heavy champion. In me, Louis H. Sullivan had a good pencil in his hand. So I then intended and still believe.

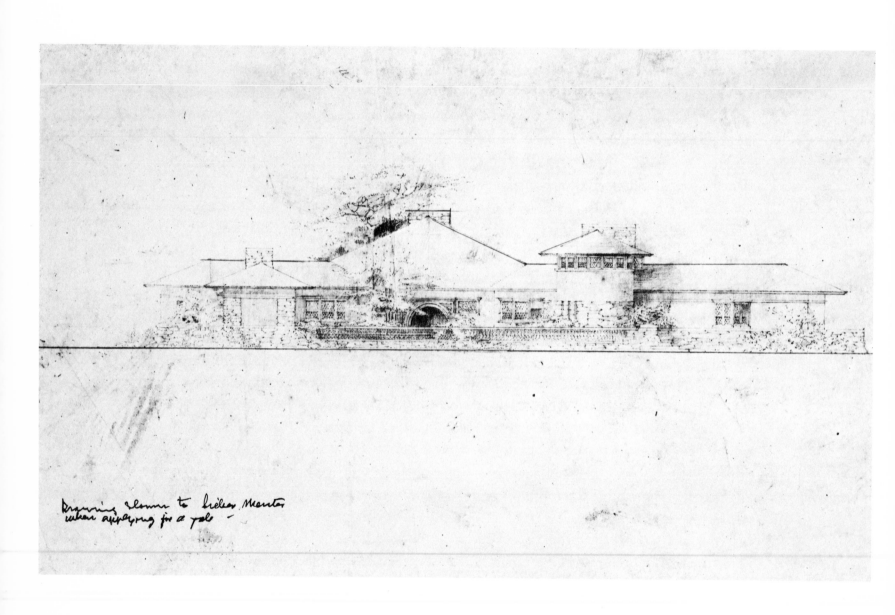

Drawing shown to Lieber Meister
when applying for a job —

"Drawing shown to Lieber Meister when applying for a job." 1888

CHAPTER TWO

BY SELF-SACRIFICE THE HONEST DISCIPLE MUST HIMSELF BEGET THE DEEPER EXPERIENCE THAT MAKES HIM MASTER

I was quite lonesome in that strange, unfriendly, daily routine of the office that would often break into open rows. So, during the first two lonely years I was in hostile office environment. To keep me company at first, and later in order to train him into lieber-meister's way with me in case anything were to happen to deprive him of my trained help, I had brought into the Adler and Sullivan office to qualify—by work under me—a young draughtsman I had known at Silsbee's: the novice Elmslie—I called him "George." He was a conscientious Scotch lad, slow of speech and movement, who had never been really "young" as he then seemed to me. His character was fine, our comradeship perfect, and some of my much too much work I now began to pass along to the faithful George.

So, when the firm moved from the Borden block to the new quarters (we had planned them for the Auditorium tower), George was alongside in my room which had the best of the wide "guillotine" windows to the east overlooking the lake: Lake Michigan. At the mas-ter's own request, this room next his was partitioned off and ceiled over for myself. The room completed the east end of the big draughting room with the continuous row of big windows to the north. His desk was visible from my big draughting table. George, who had come over to the Borden block to work, for about six years thereafter now worked at his drawing board next my own big table in this small private office in order to continue with the master should anything happen to me.

At the same time some thirty confirmed—a few peripatetic—draughtsmen, young and old, were, by now, working under me. The draughtsmen worked in the open space between my place and a similar place partitioned off at the opposite end of the tower

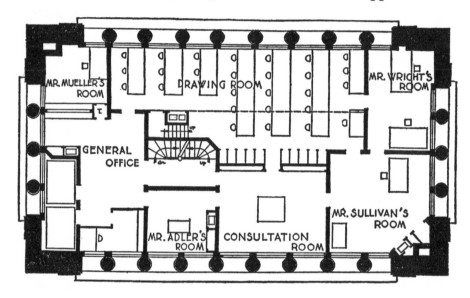

draughting room (the west end) for Paul Mueller, the young German engineer educated at Stuttgart. He was in charge of engineering drawings and the several superintendents coming daily in from the field reported to him. Tall, young Paul Mueller, the structural engineer, grew a black beard to give him more authority. He was directly under Dankmar Adler. I, with no graduation or architectural degrees to speak of as such, was not only directly under Louis H. Sullivan but more and more, because of Mr. Sullivan's absences, I was under Dankmar Adler.

This plan of the Adler and Sullivan offices in the Auditorium tower was made for the firm by myself while we were still in the old Borden block. It was later published by

Adler and Sullivan in the Engineering Record of June 7, 1890 and explains pretty well the status of work in the office at that time.

The first designs for the Auditorium were made just before I came to the office. The first studies were brick and efflorescent terra cotta—a pointed tile roof on the tower—but under the Adler influence the design had become more the severe fenestration crowned by the nobly frowning tower we now see. But the Walker wholesale—a Bedford stone structure on West Adams Street—was done while we were still in the Borden block. This building, though a prominent one, seems lost to sight as I have seldom seen it illustrated. It was a facade in Romanesque terms (not rock-face, however), an arched cut-stone structure much in keeping with the Auditorium facade and of the same Bedford stone—with a fatal defect: great twin-arches landed on a pier dividing the building in the middle. The master brought the manila stretch with the elevation penciled upon it, laid it over my board with the remark, "Wright, there is the last word in the Romanesque." I puzzled over that remark a lot. What business had he with the Romanesque? "Wright, there is the last word in Romanesque." I have never forgotten the remark.

THE GRAND OPENING

Let's say the great Auditorium is now about completed. Adelina Patti—incredibly famous then—and a long line of better than star-musicians like the Italian Tamagno, had made the opening an occasion never to be forgotten. Benjamin Harrison, the President of the United States, was present and prime promoter Peck had the President's words of praise for the great civic enterprise carved on the broad paneled wooden tablet to be put in the foyer of the Auditorium. I had been instructed to design the tablet. Promoter Peck bowed his pearl-gray top hat right and left. He, too, was enjoying his role of conquering hero. All the carping usual in every novel building enterprise had come to a timely end when the great edifice came to proof.

The "greatest" musicians' names (to myself had carelessly fallen the choice, by instinct, of "the greatest") were cast in high relief in plaster upon the side wings of the reducing curtain of the great proscenium arch. The choice (it included Berlioz) passed unchallenged—and I felt no longer uneasy. Wagner's name was there—of course—and my haphazard choice of names seemed to matter little so long as Wagner's was included. Great fame is exciting up to a certain point—a hackneyed affair beyond that point—but on the occasion of this grand opening there was the greatest outpouring of Chicago's most important and best, memorable and comparable in my mind now only to the opening about twenty-three years later of Chicago's Midway Gardens on the Plaisance just below the cast-iron Gothic of the Rockefeller Chicago University. But whole editions of local newspapers celebrated this Auditorium event. And, for weeks, there was no other compatible subject of conversation to be found. As the name of Adler and Sullivan skyrocketed to an unparalleled fame-of-the-moment, everyone connected with this establishment shone in the reflected glory of an adversely criticized great work finally come to tremendously high approval. No one who shared the occasion will ever forget the fortnight of grand opera which then came on. Opera had a new lease on Chicago life by way of this golden place in which to see and hear it. Though never myself convinced that as an art form opera was more than a ponderous anachronism, the enthusiasm now evoked was contagious and we all floated upon it like small ships in a grand pageant. The big chief walked about with his hands clutched well back under his coattails. The chief's designer was drowning the greatest success of his life but one, with his old Beaux Arts' friends and lifetime favorites Tom Healy and Louis Millet, his sympathetic "decorators" on the big project. They might be found together now at the great, wide, unique Auditorium bar, which I had to design for the great building owing to last-moment pressure on L. H. S. himself. This item may indicate how well versed in the technique of the master "his pencil" had become.

From now forward the fame of Louis H. Sullivan was secure—as one might have thought—and he seemed to be drowning the thought. It was like him.

But no fame is ever secure.

Ornament detail. Drawing by Frank Lloyd Wright. Auditorium Building, Chicago. 1887-89 **65**

Yes. A great genius had appeared in the world of architecture. His triumph was, complete. And provincial, professional envy immediately got out its dull little hatchet whetted it, and went to work on him. Disciples arose and shone.

The great room for music began to be copied everywhere. It was surely his. Sentences from his "Hymn to Nature" were blazoned in gold on a great mural surmounting the elliptical arch of the great proscenium—"The utterance of life is a song—the symphony of nature"; from other hymns of his other sentences were inscribed on poetic murals painted within the blind semicircular archways set in the great side-walls of the room. (I remember I wondered why these were circular rather than elliptical like the proscenium.) Electric lighting (at that time in infancy) was a revelation as the lights centering in relief patterns were sunk into the relief ornament of the building itself. Lighting was thus for the first time made more or less integral with the building. Hitherto, chandeliers had made of artificial lighting something added to the building: a pleasant "fixture" only. The exquisite cream-colored delicate imaginative reliefs, by the master hand, of the interior were thus high-lighted where not wholly emblazoned with gold leaf. Intricate gilded reliefs swept over the succession of elliptical arches forming the vast ceiling. Exquisitely modeled ornament was everywhere delicately glistening and dancing overhead and to be found in unexpected places almost anywhere alongside. The catenary curve of the main floor on which the audience rested wore all this as a golden aura.

Acoustics had now come to architecture. Owing to this repeated recession of elliptical arches forming the great overhead and extending from the proscenium (widest in the world) into the body of the house like a magnified trumpet, the big chief had struck a principle that created a miracle in the projection and extension of sound. To aid in this respect, the overhead arches themselves were charged with warm air flowing out from the stage toward the audience through perforated pattern in each face and soffit of the great elliptical arches. Air was thus flowing toward the audience from the source of sound to be drawn out beneath the seats under the audience. Thus sound rode along to the listeners upon air-conditioning. Air-conditioning arrived as a carrier of sound! All opposing wall surfaces to the rear of the grand room itself were deadened by soft lime-mortar an inch thick (the chief believed only in good lime-mortar for such purposes) and sand finished so as to offer no echoing reflections anywhere. Not alone had a miracle of appropriate beauty arrived but also a great triumph in acoustics. Adler and Sullivan were now authority in a field hitherto largely ruled by academic superstitition codified. In spite of the "authorities," the firm could now build all the theatres and opera houses they wanted to build. Opportunity to build them began to come along to the offices in the tower proudly rising now above all this glamorous, golden splendor.

As for these Adler and Sullivan offices—well . . . it was something in the eyes of the by-and-large to be there at all in any capacity whatsoever! Genial, bald old Weaton, office factotum with the purse (which I used often to tap between weekends), twinkled his shrewd blue eyes. The office cub, noisy Anton, hushed himself up. A new "hush" had come over the entire establishment. The lineaments of gratified desire were showing. There was less noise at the entrance, more quiet in the private rooms. Success with all her gleaming harness had moved in to awe the entourage of "Adler and Sullivan." The big chief, taking things happily as a matter of course, was there in his place as always. But the designing partner had gone south to cast off the strain of the mad rush to the finish considered fit for the grand opening. He remained away for six weeks at Ocean Springs, Mississippi, in the country house I had designed for him. The chief, meantime, came to sit and talk with me more often than usual. His generous heart and salty wisdom never seemed dearer and clearer to us all than now. The great event seemed rather to have sobered than excited him.

He was like that. His casual salutation a twinkle in his eye as he would come into my room—"Ah, Wright—I see! Still snatching victory from the jaws of defeat?"

The master was working away in his rose garden down there at Biloxi by the Gulf, next door to his beloved friends the James Charnleys for whom I had drawn a cottage which I liked better than lieber-meister's. Both were experiments that seem tame enough now. Later I designed the Charnley townhouse on Astor Street.

Well . . . who would not want to be an architect conceived in glory such as this! I suppose Alexander when he had conquered the world knew some such sense of pride.

But soon the work in the tower offices proceeded to fall back again into something like routine. The procession of commissions included not only loft buildings, skyscraper office buildings, hotels, and factories, but more theatres and opera houses. All were turned out by the "office," ready to build. In all ensuing activity the congenial partners, except for the occasional Southern interim at Biloxi, worked together like hand in glove. The office force doubled and doubled again. Many young men, later to become well-known practicing architects, moved through the scene. In particular, I remember Irving Gill of California. I had taken him on as one of my squad. Running against him some months later, when I was getting out of the elevator into the office and he was about to get in to it, I noticed my habit of hair and flowing black tie had been adopted by him. This had been the case with others often enough, but in this instance the affair suddenly seemed to me more like caricature. I regarded him for a moment and said, "Gill, for Christ's sake, get your hair cut." The common enough exhortation, to which I have myself been subjected in nearly every province of the United States, was not pleasantly said. Gill was as rank an individualist as I and he quit then and there. But his individual character came out to good purpose in the good work he did later in San Diego and Los Angeles. His work was a kind of elimination which if coupled with a finer sense of proportion would have been—I think it was, anyway—a real contribution to our so-called modern movement. There were many others no doubt giving a good account of themselves but I do not recall them now. "George," meantime, was the steady understudy alongside—a quiet non-demanding comrade. Later when I was independent he would come out to the Oak Park studio to help me when work got out of hand. A good deal of backwash accordingly got into the later buildings of the Sullivan office which was then almost solely in his charge.

As I write I see through the glass screen that cuts me off from them the Adler and Sullivan rank-and-file, sprawling over drawing boards. Familiar faces lifted occasionally, looking to see if I was looking or faces looking dreamily out of the windows—the draughtsmen. They were a small army from first to last. I sometimes wonder what became of them as I recall lieber-meister's "Wright, I have no respect at all for a draughtsman."

But, to cut this story shorter (it could go on from building to building indefinitely), the partnership under pressure of depression—and financial loss inevitable to the kind of ground-breaking work the firm was continuously doing on every job that came in—competition also keen—had made some immediate move in the direction of money, necessary. Paul Mueller had left several years before to go into partnership with a contractor, the Probst Construction Company. This grieved the big chief at the time. He had trained Mueller thoroughly. Mueller had become his man-Friday. The chief lamented him for years. First, after him, came Sickles from New York, a grandstander. The boys all looked upon him as a stuffed shirt from the McKim, Mead and White offices. Conscientious hardworking Kleinpell came next (after Sickles was confined for paresis) to take Paul Mueller's place. But the office was never the same. After Mueller left, many changes began to take place in that end of the work.

We will go forward, now, to the time when I had left the office and had been practicing building for many years—say, twenty—on my own, but, owing to a worm's-eye view I was getting of society at that moment, about out on the street myself.

CHAPTER THREE

A MASTER VENERATES ONLY TRUTH

Louis H. Sullivan venerated none except Adler, Herbert Spencer, Richard Wagner, Walt Whitman, John Edelman, and himself. I didn't know of anyone else and I don't know now whether he knew God in the depths of his heart or not. Nor did I ever hear a good word for any contemporary of his unless almost nothing for John Root. But later I discovered his secret respect, leaning a little toward envy (I was ashamed to suspect), for H. H. Richardson. Just the same and nevertheless he had liked and trusted *me* and I, loving poetry, adored the lyric poet I had instinctively felt him to be and later actually came to know as the great philosopher he was. As through the years I grew and listened to him, I learned because, though disinclined to teach at all, he would talk to me much and long about his resentments—hates—loves—of his contemporaries, of Wagner, Whitman, and his ideas of art and artists. Like his feeling toward his draughtsmen, he despised his disciples. Sometimes—forgetting me entirely—next him there in my enclosure—wide windows overlooking the vast lighted city lying peacefully by the lake—he would talk until I could arrive home on the last suburban train only way past a decent bedtime. He seemed to have found in me what he seemed to lack . . . the natural human sympathy and steadfast adoration of the young every great egoist needs. He did not like to work unless drawing designs for ornament. I think I did like to work: thanks to the farm? And soon (after a year or two) I could draw so well that later in his life "lieber-meister" sometimes failed to distinguish between my work and his own.

Meantime the designing partner, as he developed toward mastery, soon found it satisfactory—so much easier—not to draw so much himself. All architects arrive there soon or late.

POINT, LINE, AND PLANE

Beginning at the draughting board, it was my natural tendency to draw away from the mastery of his efflorescence toward the straight line and rectangular pattern, working my own rectilinear way with T-square and triangle toward the more severe rhythms of point, line, and plane. Never having been a painter I had never drawn more than a little "free-hand." So at this time not only was it my instinct to go away from free-hand exercise, but my technique (such as it was) condemned me to T-square and triangle, which I came to love and prefer, but they compelled me to stay behind the sensuous expressions the master so much loved and mastered so surpassingly well.

And by now he would sometimes reproach me, his accepted chief draughtsman.

"Wright," he would say, concerning details which I was trying (as yet by instinct) to work with T-square and triangle more simply into the materials of building construction itself, "bring it alive, man! Make it live!"

He would sit down at my board for a moment, take the "HB" pencil from my hand and, sure enough, there it would be. Alive!

"Take care of the terminals, Wright. The rest will take care of itself."

He did "make it live." And I learned to do it his way. But that extraordinary gift I somehow then regarded (do now) as peculiarly his own. I enjoyed emulation—as a challenge—and loved being useful to him in any way I could be. But no one ever had or could ever equal this, his gift, in the peculiar field that was his unique efflorescence. Where before, I ask, in surroundings so peculiarly poetry-crushing (or, for that matter, in felicitous circumstances either) was there ever a man who *out of himself* devised a complete beautiful language of self-expression as complete in itself as Wagner's music or the period ornamentation of any of the great styles which time took so many ages to perfect? The Sullivanian philosophy, so far as it was personal to him, is written in that chosen language of his most clearly and if you are going to read *him* at all, it is there to be read at level best. Not in the remarkable buildings built by the firm nor in his own writings (so I felt then and now think) were the perfect expressions of Louis H. Sullivan to be found. As I could see even then, the buildings were often far from it. His writing at that time (let's mention "Inspiration—A Spring Song," which he read to me) seemed to me a kind of "baying at the moon," as I once risked telling him with no good results where I was concerned. Or where he was concerned either. So I seldom read what he wrote. There was no need. He would sometimes read passages to me or, better still, talk about himself in his own way. Probably "trying it out on the 'pup' "? But always I preferred his drawings. Naturally enough, because I shared in them. He may have been ridiculous when he wrote: I didn't know. He was miraculous when he drew. I always wanted him to "*draw*"! But soon he began to draw less and less.

As for his literary "tastes"—he loved Walt Whitman's "Leaves of Grass" and read Herbert Spencer. Early in my life with him he gave me Spencer and Walt Whitman to read. Not so strange a pair to draw to as one might think. I read enough to show me the color of the particular tub of dye that was the Spencerian synthetic philosophy and threw the book away. But I loved Whitman although I preferred Bach—and Beethoven especially— to Wagner. Most of all I *preferred* that he "draw." I never had occasion to be ashamed of myself with him then.

CHAPTER FOUR

OF THE GROUND, NOT ON IT

In any honest search for an ideal to stand firm against the "classic" (or "exterior") ideal—that inspires the super-elegance of Greek art by aiming at contrast to nature and becoming the servile pseudo-classic of our day—were we to search among the expressions of the interior (or organic) ideal as anciently set forth by Laotze, Moti, Jesus, and the Buddha (more recently by poet-philosophers like Shakespeare, Cervantes, Unamuno, Whitman, Emerson, Thoreau, Nietzsche, Goethe, Rousseau, Mark Twain, Melville, Lecomte du Noüy and so many others), a high place in modern times should inevitably go to Louis H. Sullivan.

As a complete expression of himself the master left to us not only printed volumes expounding his philosophy, but by his own more enhancing terms in his own drawings as he collected, signed, and dated them himself—reproduced here for the first time. In these little masterpieces of poetic imagination, the poet in him shines forth on the record as a free, independent spirit characteristic of the free of all time. Why could his own time only pass him by? But a handsome folio was published in his lifetime by the A. I. A. at the instigation of a friend of his named Whitaker. The prophet of a democratic architecture was recognized under the imprint of his own profession. But, too late for him. Claude Bragdon, an enthusiastic, sincere disciple of the master, had also been trying to get his writing printed in his lifetime but without success.

This work published by the A. I. A. might well have been called his last will and testament but should never be. The drawings I have used here as illustration by his own bequest—and implied request—bear eloquent witness to whatever I have said of him or could say. The publication of these poignantly beautiful rhythms tardily fulfills the promise I made to him. Even then the trembling hand with its nicotine-stained forefinger, his heart pounding, recovering for a moment, would regain much of the perfect poise, push, and touch of former days. This ornament was his unquenchable gift! The drawings he made for the late work published by the A. I. A.—though less spontaneous—show but little falling off from the power and grace of the performances included here, made when I knew him at the height of his power. But as you will see they are no longer so spontaneous. The beloved master was illustrating a "thesis." The earlier drawings he gave to me are dated by him—and, out of so many, I have chosen the few I think he would have chosen himself.

Not until toward the end of my service to Adler and Sullivan did I perceive that the nature of materials meant no more to lieber-meister than their nature had meant to the ancient Greeks but with a nameless difference. Materials, all alike, were only grist for the marvelous sensuous rhythmic power of imagination he possessed. His spirit was deeply involved in the fluent organic expressions of form naturally appropriate to a plastic—and clay was (it is forever) the ideal "plastic." But, whether executed in stone, wood, or iron, all materials were "clay" in the master's hands and—well—that was enough? Because of this effulgent sense of sympathy he possessed—for all he cared or anything he seemed to want to know materials were pretty much all *one* to him. In the primal plastic—clay—his opulent imagery could triumph, and did so. As might have been the case with the Greeks had they the gift he had. But this inconsistency by its very constancy began to disturb me. Not much at first but an uneasy little. More and more, though, as years went by I would instinctively draw toward expressions more appropriate to other building materials by way of T-square and triangle: just as purely instinctively rhythmic—so it seemed to me—but more architectural ones. Or so I thought. I now know that "architectural" is not exactly the right word because the basis of architectural thought was there in what he did, but I know now that many a long lifetime must be spent to find the proper technique—each man for himself—to put into actual building practice the implications of the great philosophy to which the lyric poet dedicated himself in this sensuous efflorescence so peculiarly and absolutely his own. But if a building was ever to be organic in the same sense that this deeply individual expression of himself was so and prophesied it, this lifetime, at least, is only a beginning. I felt this rather than knew it—then. Now I realize it and acknowledge it.

Nevertheless, given a novel problem of that moment—like the troublesome sky-scraper—his fine mind instantly saw its chief characteristic. *Aware of its nature* he got its real sense. It was tall! Why not, then, nobly tall instead of a simpering super-imposition of several or many low buildings to arrive at height in the manner that "skyscrapers" were being practiced by his contemporaries? By all except one: John Root. Root's Monadnock was a noble building. It was later but even further along. The Wainwright went very far— a splendid performance on the record for all time. Although the frontal divisions were still artificial, they were at least, and at last, effective. But the flat roof-slab overhung the street, you say? Well, you may also say that these frontal divisions were no less eclecticisms for being fresh. But a new countenance had come to light! He had conceived it as still a column, as I came to see many years later. Base, shaft, and capital were there with no direct or apparent relation to actual construction. The picturesque verticality with which he did emphasize its height, although appropriate, was still a mere facade. Where and how was the actual nature of this building construction? Equivocation in this respect by the Wainwright. Yes, but far less than in most contemporary building effort. This revolt and departure from the insignificant academicisms of that day wore a genuinely fresh countenance and was prophetic if not profound. As he threw the "stretch," with the first three bays outlined in pencil upon it, I sensed what had happened. In his vision, here beyond doubt, was the dawn of a new day in skyscraper architecture. The "countenance" then was all anyone ever thought to ask of any building anyway. I never heard the master once refer to Greek architecture, but again see the Greeks, see Richardson, see the painter-architects of the Renaissance. See the stencilists' cliché of today. See them all for five centuries previous and past! Look back and see the interminable vistas of interior structure ignored or falsified in exteriors without any sense of the nature of the problem as you see a type in the Wainwright. But other lifetimes yet to come would have to be expended upon the task of making the countenance of building authentic of structure—in order to finally make that countenance of construction integral: innate architecture. We can honestly call only an organic type of performance the new architecture of this era that I am calling organic. I "felt" this then. I realize it now because he was then what he was.

Yes. It is only fair to say, now, that in none of these Adler and Sullivan buildings are "form and function" one or, excepting clay (called "terra cotta"), is the nature-of-materials considered at all either as a matter of fact or, as determining organic form. But the buildings if considered on their own in time and place went so far beyond contemporaries in point of enlightened countenance as to prophesy a new integrity so far in advance of the work of the period as to arrest the sentient passer-by with prescience of a new world.

Perhaps, owing to a long line of ministerial primogeniture and later a frugal Unitarian upbringing, I was quick to appreciate and adore this "unitarian" aspect of simplicity. But, never yet satisfied with simplicity as "exterior" (in two dimensions only"), I longed to see the thing go through and "button at the back," become genuinely unitarian. But how? The then still-mysterious third dimension was essential. Or to come through from within and button at the front would do as well, if that was any easier. And though the master so spoke and practiced when designing his ornament, the buildings the firm did were seldom far along the road of organic character until they were compared with the buildings of the robust Romanist in "rock-face"—H. H. Richardson. Richardson was the grand exteriorist and what a commotion *he* created! In the later Adler and Sullivan days more and more often in mischief my "T-square and furtive triangle"—steadier now—began to push a little here and there into the few things that circumstances left to me. Push in the direction which I *felt* (not then knowing) was Nature worship—out of which was to come "in-the-nature-of-materials," not yet clear to me. The technique of that interior philosophy of materials was then more instinct than knowledge where I was concerned.

But I continued experience in that direction by means of a more rectilinear and obvious schematic abstraction—which I felt and later thought suited to the machine—wherever I could do so.

It was my good luck that the refusal of the firm to build residences gave me a number of important chances like the urban Charnley House which I did at home "overtime" for the firm. It helped pay debts due to the excess cost of the "funny little house." At this time let the Charnley dwelling on Astor Street stand as instance. There were others like MacHargs', the master's own house, and his brother Albert's—all not so good. But now the machine began to push into my consciousness—to come out later when I began to work for myself.

By a little here and a little there beneath his livelier more expressive manner, without knowing it, I was corrupting his work as in that eclecticism—the Wainwright tomb at St. Louis, the Schiller Building, the Stock Exchange, Chicago, the Meyer Building which lost its cornice, and some minor things on which his hand had no time to dwell. Or should I say I was "interrupting" results as he would have had them? He did better when he would go all the way alone, as it would be easy for me to point out in the executed work. The amateur hand shows in details that the master would have done better—otherwise.

Yes, the significant implication of lieber-meister's gift to me was his practice "*of—the thing—not—on—it*," which I recognized and saw most clearly realized in his unique sense of ornament. Seeing this in his use of clay, when modeled under his supervision from the plastic mud itself, was always to me a prophecy and sheer joy. His sentient integral modulation by imaginative reason proceeding from generals to particulars always inspired me, as it must inspire anyone who can see into it as he drew it—or read the record when his designs were modeled as he wished them modeled. If he attended to the modeling himself (he usually did): perfection! His own soul's philosophy incarnate. Music its only paraphrase and peer.

Nevertheless and because of this music, in course of time I grew eager to go further. The matter had now ceased to be Louis H. Sullivan or Frank Lloyd Wright with me: not the aim of his gift or mine but of the giver. I began to ask myself—why not this eternal principle harmonizing any and every building anywhere with environment and for every purpose? Why not the edifice symphonic throughout from footing to coping of the *structure* itself—a harmony like music? My father taught me that a symphony was an *edifice* of sound. I wanted to see, someday, a building continuously plastic from inside to outside, and exterior from outside to inside. No stopping anywhere once the eternal "principle" prophesied anew by him so clearly in the immediate field of his symphonic eloquence was recognized. Assertion of pure form as *integral* rhythmic movement was what made him a lyric poet. Almost all ornamentation up to and especially in the time in which he worked— had degenerated to mere applied surface decoration. Ornament was "appliqué"—even as lace curtains are hung. From the first, "*of-the-thing-not-on-it*" was inimical to the thought and the way of our times. But I saw it as the norm of creative work of all and every kind. It was that *quality* in him which fired my imagination. Perhaps because the "interior" character of his sense of "efflorescence" gibed with my own wrestle with nature circumstance out there on the farm? It was square with the *unit*-arianism of my old Welsh grandfather. The Froebel kindergartening my mother discovered at the Centennial, and herself took to give to me, pointed that way. All this background now came forward a step and began to "click." The letters my mother wrote at the time—"Keep close to earth, my boy, and should you have to choose between truth and success, be sure to choose truth." This probably helped. So the philosophy of which Louis H. Sullivan was now champion was not Greek to me in that early day but easily prophetic. He must live up to it always. I will help him do it—I thought. Arrogance? Yes. You see—even so early not humble. Well "I have not yet so much to be humble about."

A gentle war thus came up and went on over ways and means. I sat in on some of the last moments of this war between the rapidly developing master and the impatient curiosity of an enthusiastic, developing "pencil in his hand." The designing partner grew more frequently absent or disinterested and this was more and more license for the T-square and triangle I now wielded as second nature. Both became a great opportunity for the eager, egoistic novice that I was. Great sensuousness to form and especially integration—the "third dimension" as integer—gradually began to come clearer, not only useful but why not vital in the creative employment of all materials in all the arts? I was growing up beside the master to see them that way—that's all, and thanks be to himself. But the machine kept worrying me. The master hadn't mentioned it and I didn't until I was on my own. At Hull House I brought the matter to a head in "The Art and Craft of the Machine," a paper I wrote and read there.

When these rare but steadily increasing chances to experiment came my way, I made (I suppose I stole them) continual minor ones. Some were disastrous: riding hard on my conscience then. I did not know (nor do I know now) how much of this thing was wrong. The master did sometimes disapprove. He would reproach me, occasionally, and sometimes too I was in deep trouble with the chief himself as in the height of windowsills in the Schiller Building which I raised six inches to get the plastic flow of the surrounding frames complete. There were other devastating details there is no need to mention. Anshe Maariv is still there in Chicago on South Michigan Avenue to attest the folly of the experiments I made in violent changes of scale in actual building construction as I had seen lieber-meister practice it in ornament with startling success.

But the magic element of plasticity—which is what this attempt at exposition amounts to—I believed to be the property in building I was capable of using someday. Just as surely, integrity of form and idea was the great need of our time if the phase of his philosophy that I could absorb was sound. Here was the practical way to give integrity to anything of useful beauty or beautiful use in life on this earth. If beauty in this mortal phase of our lives is ever to be the fine morality or happy result of conscious human effort. Give all the forms of our civilization organic integrity and you will save ours from the periodic destruction overtaking all other civilizations. This I grew to believe then. I believe it now more strongly than ever.

But need for salvation by proper use of the machine came clearer to me then as my turn to build on my own drew near, and it was my first thought when I began to practice.

So I began to study the *Nature* of things more and more and "all down the line." What was the Nature of this machine we must use, above all? Why not use it creatively as an artist's tool! Everything everywhere—not only in building—true to the ground and nature of materials but true as well to the new tools and new methods that produced the thing. In due course if buildings were so built the thought in them would change the ugly circumstances under which we were all living—even react and ennoble the purpose for which the buildings were built. Buildings react for good or ill upon the human lives lived in them more directly than church, school, or state. Buildings are a synthesis of society and civilization in a system of philosophy and ethics, if they are organic architecture.

This unitarian (transcendental?) train of thought, getting into architecture, found in the suggestions of Louis H. Sullivan's philosophy as it came through his theory of ornament, made effective impact upon my own upbringing. The consequences are still in action and the end is not yet.

Many years later as I lived, drew, and built I found in what I conceived and drew that the element I now called plasticity (the master had rendered it so completely in clay) carried in its own nature implications of unexplored structural continuity and could exemplify, simplify, and even prove the *aesthetic* validity of structural forms themselves. This *innate* or organic property of all form, if not merely looked *at* but looked *into* as structure, absorbed me soon after I had left my work with the "firm." This absorbs me now and will absorb the more sentient young mind in architecture for centuries to come. Plastic continuity is a product of these instructive spatial properties implicit in the work emanating from his own beautiful drawings. These drawings were his genuine, deepest enjoyment. So far as they went they were the embodiment of the philosophy personal to him. As I look back upon it I can see the drawings were no less truly graph of the ancient philosophy of Laotze, Jesus, or the thought of great moderns like Walt Whitman, Unamuno, Nietzsche, Goethe, Victor Hugo, Bach, Beethoven, and the integrity of so many of the early Germans, Spaniards, and Italians, Chinese, Japanese, and (yes, for that matter) all the spirits loving honor and sincerely serving to express it in work from the beginning of time.

We have unwittingly passed by many great sayers and doers whose music or painting or poetry is still fallow in the great "in-betweens" of universal knowledge that is poetry, yet unidentified but nevertheless someday to speak out what lieber-meister's own eager enjoyment with his pencil was saying to me when he drew. But, not in buildings, because if buildings had ever been built accordingly we could not have passed them by. We would not now be compelled to originate our own in changed and changing circumstances. Buildings that became architecture in this interior sense would be the incontestable record of man's culture in his own time. A little of it has clung through the ages to various buildings. So it is still truth universal that shines forth in the life of these rhythmic developments of surface. Yes, when conceived in plastic material like clay and modeled beneath the touch of sympathetic sentient fingers at his express command, Sullivanian ornament was not only a fresh emotional phase of inner rhythm in his own name but prophecy. Therefore his drawings are not alone lyric poems but as a matter of course they perfectly illustrate the *universality* of the philosophy the master loved, declared, and to which I—the novice— wholeheartedly subscribed as it flowed from beneath his magic "touch."

Subsequent years flew by.

As my work went on, gradually, I saw more clearly the spiritual implications of plasticity where space was a quality to be realized in building construction. I learned the stimulating values of its implication wherever the life of the free individual might be served by the building. Of course, such objective outward expression of subjective inner life can only survive in the freedom of genuine democracy; the highest form of aristocracy ever seen—that of the innate aristocrat, aristocracy not hereditary but of the man himself— as himself. Inspiration for the way of building appropriate to that inner man is what came to me by way of my own choice of direct apprenticeship to a great master. I believe voluntary apprenticeship of that kind is the way an artist-to-be can really become an architect in his own right. He can learn most from one who *is* himself an architect. But I remember that sometimes (emotionally impatient in those latter days) I would ask myself, "Doesn't 'lieber-meister' know his own when he sees it?," although my "better nature" would obtain and I would stay on pretty well in line, though doing work out of hours for some friends to whom I had occasion to feel grateful. But the master was compelled by various pressures to leave more and more to the voluntary apprentice as the years went by. Sometimes the "argument"—if such it were—would come my way by his own default. Then I would try to practice in structure by way of point, line, and plane the rhythms that he preached so well in the plastic clay whenever he was completely free of the complex restraints of the actual building process. Could I wait? During this seventh year with him I began to be impatient now and then—sometimes he with me. There was but a short time to go to complete the five-year term of my lawyer-contract but I felt I owed him too much even to think of wanting to leave him: owing him as much then as now the master owes to me. A statement unbecoming? But only due in course of that "plastic continuity" of human relationship which should be the natural accession and succession of "pencil" to master if the relationship is right; or of discipleship to masterhood, if honest. But I was rudely to awaken to the fact that my status was neither. I was just a draughtsman.

Circumstances do not wait. The "funny little house" was already paid for and the deed due from the firm. I asked for the deed only to be surprised by refusal from Mr. Sullivan. Why? "Read your contract, Wright. I have seen the house you are doing for Dr. Harlan. Your contract expressly forbids doing work outside office hours." I read the contract. It did. My assumption was that, if I could plan houses at home for the firm to pay my debts without impairing my usefulness to my employers, I could go on with it. But I now saw that was juvenile and probably dishonest. Had I stolen the Harlan house from the firm? This put me on bad terms with myself. There were other similar sins the master hadn't mentioned. I appeared before him to argue the case—instead of to confess frankly and apologize, as I should have done. This angered him and, being so manifestly in the wrong myself, angered me. I reacted like any other draughtsman—as a matter of fact, I was. Like Weatherwax, I threw down my pencil, turned my back on the master, and walked away never to go back to him again. He had never talked to me in that tone of voice before. The deed duly followed from the hand of the chief. This deed in my hand and having read the contract, I wanted to go back not to resume work but to apologize and confess a grave fault to the master. Swallowing my shame hard I went back to see him. I was astonished to hear him say, "Wright, your conduct has been so perfidious there is nothing I care to hear you say." I was cut back and down in the very flower of my relationship to him. Inasmuch as I saw the fault as only taking too much for granted, I felt surely this was exaggeration. I went home, my shame doubled. Although I often felt drawn to him in following years, I never went near him after that. It was nearly twenty years before I saw him again. This bad end to a glorious relationship has been a dark shadow to stay with me the days of my life.

You see, when I signed that contract I became a draughtsman. Now he was treating me like one. The fact is I was facing the fact that facts are facts. A case where the fact was far from the truth.

CHAPTER FIVE

THE BREAKUP OF THE FIRM

Sometime after the destruction of Taliesin I—about 1919—lieber-meister and I came together again.

Returning from work on the Imperial in Japan, I found things had not been going so well with him. Since the breakup of the firm, separation from Dankmar Adler several years after that triumphant disaster to American architecture the Columbian "Fair," had left him to carry on alone in the tower offices. The Guarantee Building, Buffalo, had just come into the office when I left. This building was the last one built under the Adler and Sullivan partnership, but a group of minor bank buildings went on afterward under his aegis by way of the faithful George.

To go back to the earlier years of Adler and Sullivan history: owing to the nature of such creative work as theirs Adler and Sullivan, Architects, had made little or no money. Their work cost them as much, often more, than they ever received for it, although they were paid as well as any first-class architects of that time—probably better paid than most. The depression following the great success of the Columbian Fair therefore hit the firm of Adler and Sullivan particularly hard. At this psychological moment Richard Crane, the magnate owner of the Crane Company, manufacturers of pipe and plumbing, came along as tempter. As a client his respect for Adler was boundless and now he offered Dankmar

Adler, Architect, $25,000 a year to sell Crane elevators. (About $75,000 now?) In a fit of despondency the chief accepted. Some money had to be earned by someone. Sullivan, left alone in the tower offices, was resentful.

As a matter of course the clientele had been mostly Adler's, as Sullivan now had reason to know. Louis H. Sullivan, Architect, soon faced the fact that he was where he must take what was left to him from the Adler connection and start to build a practice for himself. Only one Adler and Sullivan client stayed on with lonely Sullivan: Mayer, of Schlesinger and Mayer. Dave Mayer employed him to design his new retail store building on State Street, Chicago. I remember the master's sense of outrage because Uncle Dan— D. H. Burnham (make no little plans)—by tactics usual to the profession—had tried to take this commission away from him.

Meantime, as I got the story, a curious mishap had befallen Crane's new lion. The chief duly went to New York to sell Crane elevators for the new Siegel Cooper Building. The opposing bidder, Sprague Electric, simply pulled out a report Adler the architect had made concerning their elevator as proposed for use in the Auditorium Building some years previous. It gave the Electric everything—yes, including the Siegel Cooper work. Mr. Adler came home. Some words from Crane. The big chief was unused to be talked to in that tone of voice, especially from a man who had hitherto come to him for justice or for favors. The result of the interview was a cheque from Crane to Adler for $25,000—a year's salary, and a contract canceled.

All now hoped to see the two partners together again. But no, the master was still resentful. The big chief had had enough, he said.

As yet I had not once communicated with Mr. Sullivan since I had left the firm. Sometime later Mr. Adler, now much at the Union League Club, called me. I went to talk things over with him. The old chief seemed morose. He had been greatly worried by the risks he had taken to please his clients: in the matter of the added height of the tower (three times) to please Mr. Sullivan; in certain other features of the Auditorium Building, such as the addition of the banquet hall over the steel trusses that spanned the big auditorium itself, to please his client Peck. It was the addition to the height of the tower (ingeniously reinforcing the foundations) to please Sullivan that was causing most concern. In the affair of the addition of the banquet hall over the trusses spanning the big Auditorium movement had not yet stopped. The settlement of the side-walls into which the steel cantilever beams were set, (carrying the cast-iron box-fronts between them like something between the points of a pair of closing shears), would sometimes crack the cast-iron shells of these box-fronts with reports like cannon going off. The tower itself was still settling, causing cracks in adjoining portions of the building. There never was real danger. Collapse was impossible but the continuous movements caused some damage and more talk. This situation Adler had to bear. No doubt a great humiliation to him.

When I came to see him at his invitation I noticed a great change in the old chief. He was thinner; seemed unhappy. For the first time I heard him speak bitterly of his partner who, it seemed, had published the Guarantee Building of Buffalo, New York, with Adler's name deleted from the plans. This act seemed to hurt the old chief terribly.

"But for me, Wright, there never would have been a Guarantee Building."

"But, Mr. Adler," I said, "I am sure you will find there's some mistake. You will find the omission was not Mr. Sullivan's fault; probably the publisher's. Why don't you make sure?"

"I'm sure enough, Wright," he said.

But I tried him in and out concerning his former partner; pleaded the master's case with him. Told him truly how much and where there was such great disappointment over their separation—we all believed each needed the other. If ever two men did, they did—had done such great work together—the depression we were in couldn't last; and many private arguments I thought I knew for resuming the old relationship. It was all useless. I was impotent.

Thrusting his head forward, his gray beard in characteristic fashion down on his chest, looking out at me from under shaggy eyebrows, "No, Wright, I am going to keep my office in my hat now so far as I can. There's nothing in the big office with its big rent and a big salary list. I'll do the few buildings I can do, and instead of earning fifty thousand, keeping one thousand, I'll earn, by myself, five thousand and keep two thousand."

Looking at me again sharply, deep-set eyes under shaggy eyebrows: "Wright, take this from me, you do the same. Keep your office in your hat so far as you can!"

He added, "No architect on that individual basis ever needs a partner."

I saw that something that had lived between the two men—who so needed each other always and even more so now—had already burned out. Again a world of high thought and fine feeling had come to a tragic end.

We walked over from the Union League to the several small rooms the chief had taken on the Wabash Avenue side of the Auditorium, while his partner—now alone—was still carrying on up in the old offices of the tower. A heartbreaking situation. But I still believed they would come together.

I said this when I left—feeling utterly futile. Worry and disappointment had already done something to the grand old chief. This was no way of life for him.

In a short time he was dead.

I have never regretted taking his advice.

Many years later (about twenty after I had left him), with no communication between us meantime, the master and I met again in response to a telephone call from him. Friends of both had urged me to go and see him. I saw instantly that he too had gone from reported bad to far worse than I could imagine. Going to the Auditorium management I found they had finally refused to carry him further in the splendid tower offices—offered him two rooms below, next those Adler had formerly occupied on the Wabash Avenue front. He had accepted, but now a few years later even those were closed to the master. It was on that occasion that he had called me over long-distance.

I was in deep trouble myself but, luckily, able to reinstate him. Bad habits engendered by his early life in Paris had gone on and on to finally make havoc with him. Caffeine had added to his distress and now he had come to bromides. His physician said his heart was bulging between his ribs. He had "gone off," as they say, frightfully.

Notwithstanding all this havoc, he was much softened and deepened too, I thought. He gently called me "Frank." I loved the way the word came from him because before that I had heard always only "Wright."

Even now neither his courage nor his hope had gone. His were not of the going kind. His eyes burned as brightly as ever. The old gleam of humor would come into them, flicker and go. He was breaking up. His carriage was that of an old man. The body was disintegrating; his heart irretrievably damaged. But his spirit was unchanged.

I remember sitting on his desk noticing how in contrast to former neatness it was littered with dusty material-samples and old useless papers. There were some photographs of the small bank buildings he had been doing—the best one at Owatonna, Minnesota—except for the addition of the side-wing. There were other small banks. But these were tainted with backwash and showed only pitiful remnants of the great genius that flashed from him in the old days in the tower. I saw he had been leaning heavily on George Elmslie who was still with him at the time these last buildings were being done. But for George at this time he could have done little or nothing. Loyal George! I succeeded in getting the master reinstated again but the Auditorium agents were annoyed by him and wanted him out. I saw that, too.

But he was at least safe in an armchair by a fireside. He was made a life member of the Cliff Dwellers, a congenial Chicago "club" founded by D. H. Burnham and Hamlin Garland and in which I was myself a charter member. It is one of the great virtues of that organization that it did this for him.

Some years earlier I had corresponded with him a little while I was in Japan, and later from Los Angeles. Whenever I got to Chicago I took a room for him at the Congress next mine. But Wallace Rice had got him a room in a hotel on the South Side and he was now staying at the old Hotel Warner way down on Cottage Grove Avenue: an old haunt of his own also, with but little else to recommend it. A loyal little henna-haired milliner came often to see him there and so did the several young men who idolized him. He had taken great pride in the performance of the Imperial Hotel, volunteered to write articles concerning it for the Architectural Record. "At last, Frank," he said, "something they can't take away from you." I wonder why he thought "they" couldn't take it away from me? "They" can take anything away from anybody.

Several architects in Chicago also befriended him. They had been kind to him. Andrew Rebori, Max Dunning, and there was Gates of the American Terra Cotta Company, and Lucas, Hottinger, and others of the Northwestern Terra Cotta Company. Both manufacturers had especially good reasons to befriend him. Terra cotta in him had found a prophet! But he was no more tolerant of his contemporaries in architecture now than ever before. Rather less so. And much of the bitterness I have penned here concerning the disciple, as I too have seen him, fell from his own lips then with even less patience.

Because his personal habits had given professional jealousy and provincial prejudice a chance to "view with alarm" or to "dislike and deplore," though the matter involved was no concern of theirs nor—in the earlier days of his need—too much connected with his efficiency as an architect, for many years he, the master, all but starving, had been compelled to see great opportunities for work he could do so much better as to make comparison absurd—cruelly getting by him to go to inferior men. Competitors or disciples. A genius? Yes—well, that term was enough. It damned him, as it was intended to do by the lesser men who used the term to scare the sheep. "Genius"—the word will write any man off the heedless scene we live in and by huddling the sheep in alarm give work rightfully his to those who imitate him.

Money? Tiptoe to the banker to put it away when the word genius comes through! That bogeyman will get you, and failure push you around.

But by now lieber-meister was actually far gone—finally impaired, yes—much by himself. He had increasingly sought refuge from loneliness, frustration, and the petty betrayals of the professional life he detested—now driven where and as so many of his gifted brothers have been heedlessly driven by themselves since time ever was.

Nevertheless, had gracious opportunity really opened, even thus late in his life he might have been saved for some years of remarkable usefulness. But popular timidity and popular prejudice encouraged by the jealousy of his "respectable" professional contemporaries had built a wall of myth around about him so high that their timid ignorance kept his countrymen from wanting to know him. His countrymen might only have wasted him had they known him. I believe he was timely but too soon. At times despondency would overcome his natural pride and buoyancy. Even his high courage would give way to fear for his continued livelihood. Then all would clear and come up again. But only for a little while. It was at this time that he gave me the drawings you see reproduced here and said, "Frank, you will be writing about these someday?" A question in his swift glance.

But he was still caustic when in the mood, was the old master. A dozen or so of his more "successful" contemporaries would come tumbling from their perches top-side down, seamy-side out. His blade could cut and flash as it cut, even to the very last.

Some long time before all this disability closed in upon him, from his chair at the Cliff Dwellers he had been continuing the writing of "The Autobiography of an Idea." He would occasionally read a chapter to me. He had always loved to write. There, completely shut off from his natural medium of expression, he had turned more and more from the pencil to the pen. Soon he was the master there. The book meant life to him now. That I saw, and he was eagerly looking forward to the first copy from the press.

He had visited Taliesin, some years before, but the visit proved a strenuous experience for him—a bad cold was the result. Now (years later) his breath was shorter and shorter. After several cups of strong coffee he loved too much (impatient, he would pound the table if coffee was delayed), his breath was so short he would have to take my arm to walk—even very slowly. At the street crossings to step up from the street level to the sidewalk would make him pause for breath.

So I continued to see him oftener than every week if I could. But I was myself desperately involved otherwise at that dreadful time. I too was getting the worm's-eye view of society.

Some weeks passed. A telephone call to Taliesin from the Hotel Warner. I immediately took the train for Chicago and found the Warner place up in arms against him. He had now fallen worse than sick. Spells of violence came over him more and more often. This time I made peace with the manager—after raising Cain over the condition I found his room in. The manager was really devoted to Sullivan as he said he was, but he was now at his wit's end. We finally got a nurse who would stay. His devoted comrade, the little henna-haired milliner who understood him and could do almost anything with him, was absent. She herself was in the hospital at the time. She had kept in faithful touch with him.

"Don't leave me, Frank," he begged. "Stay."

I stayed and he seemed to be himself again toward evening. We talked about his forthcoming book, "The Autobiography of an Idea." He hoped there might be some income in it—for him. Hope—always hope.

I saw that he had everything to make him comfortable. So, late that evening after he had fallen asleep, I went back to Taliesin again with a promise from the nurse to call me if I were needed.

In town a few days later, I went to see him again.

He seemed better. There—at last—the first bound copy of the "Autobiography"! The book had just come in and was lying on the table by his bed. He wanted to get up. I helped him, put my overcoat round his shoulders as he sat on the bed with his feet covered up on the floor. He looked over at the book.

"There it is, Frank."

I was sitting by him, my arm around him to keep him warm and steady him. I could feel every vertebra in his backbone as I rubbed my hand up and down his spine to comfort him; and I could feel his enlarged heart pounding.

"Give me the book! The first copy to you, Frank! A pencil?" He couldn't lift his arm. Gave it up with an attempt to smile.

I could never regard the book without a strange resentment. I know it only by what he read to me himself. It had failed him as I had failed him. It was too late to do him any good. The copy he gave me was soon lost, later, in the tragic destruction of Taliesin II, and I was out on the street. But I am able to read it now and someday I will.

But yes—he the master was still there. Was he cursing a little? Gently enough. His eyes were still deeper in their wan sockets, but still burning bright. He joked about the end he saw now, and—under his breath—something. For the first time he would admit to himself that the end was near. But to me he looked as though he were better notwithstanding that helpless arm. But the man in him seemed indifferent. He didn't want to talk about it anymore, either way. Life had been pretty hard on him. Such friends as he had could do but little to make up for the deep tragedy of his frustration as the greatest architect of his time. But his ornament was his inextinguishable gift to the last and he had thrust the drawings you see here into my hands several days before when he was all but dying.

I had passed through many situations with him that looked worse than this one. So I put him back to bed again—covered him up—and sat there by him on the edge of the bed. He fell asleep. Another crisis had apparently passed. He seemed to be sleeping well, to breathe deeply enough and more easily. Once more. The nurse stepped out for a moment. An imperative call for me came in—a tragic crisis at Taliesin! I left a note for the nurse to call me immediately if there was any change in him for the worse.

At Taliesin, in the midst of disgraceful commotion, I listened anxiously for the telephone. No call coming through, I felt reassured.

But the day after the next I learned of the death of the master from the newspapers. A long-distance call from Max Dunning said that he died the day after I left him.

Several architects, warm-hearted little Max Dunning one of them, happened to come just at the end to see him and they had taken charge.

The master had nothing left in the world that he could call his own but the new clothes it had been a pleasure of my life to see him in—these and a beautiful old daguerreotype of his lovely mother, himself and his brother, aged about nine, seen standing on either side of her. These were his only worldly possessions.

Knowing he was dying he had given the prized daguerreotype to the nurse to give to "Frank."

His few remaining friends picked up his body, planned a funeral at Graceland Cemetery at which Wallace Rice, his crony at the Cliff Dwellers, spoke. I attended but stayed outside. Later "they" designed a monument for him . . . a slab of ornament designed by George Elmslie in the master's own vein to put upon his grave: the young understudy I had brought over to Sullivan from Silsbee's because the master wanted me to train someone to take my place in case anything should happen to me. George had taken my place when I left. He was faithful to the master and stayed on with him ten years or more. But to me, who had loved the master—and loving him was understanding him—this idea of imitating his work as a monument to him was worse than ironic. There was nothing to be done about it worth doing. It was his friends' best thought for the man now, and no monument is ever more than a monument to those who erect it. Is it?

By the eternal. These indecent exposures we call monuments! Will we never make an end of them? Such banality (profanity—the word nearer the truth) as they represent in our country!

But what great man ever lived whose memory was not traduced, made ridiculous, or unwittingly insulted by the *monument* "they" erected to their sense of themselves in his name after he was dead? Abraham Lincoln and Thomas Jefferson again to mind. Such monuments are made by those who, voluntarily or not, never did anything but betray the thing the great man they professed to honor loved most. Those "friends" who were charitable when he was in need; officious when he died. By a gravestone—seeking to be on good terms with themselves at his expense now that he is dead.

I wrote something in the fullness of my heart at the time, to be published somewhere. I forget where. This is it. A funeral "oration"? I suppose so. But, such as it was, my farewell to lieber-meister:

THE MASTER'S WORK

The new in the old and old in the new is ever principle.

Principle is all and single the reality the beloved master, Louis Sullivan, ever loved. It gave to the man stature and to his work true significance.

His loyalty to principle was the more remarkable as *vision* when all around him poisonous cultural mists hung low to obscure or blight any bright hope of finer beauty in the matter of this world.

The buildings he has left with us for a brief time are the least of him. In the heart of him he was of infinite value to the countrymen who wasted him not because they would; but because *they could not know him.*

Any work, great as human expression, must be studied in relation to the time in which it insisted upon its own virtues and got itself into human view.

So it is with the work he has left to us.

Remember, you who can, the contemporaries of the Chicago Auditorium, his first great building.

They were the hectic Pullman Building, W. W. Boyington's chamfered "Board of Trade," the hideous Union Station and many other survivors in the idiom of that harsh, insensate period.

Outside the initial impetus of John Edelman in his early days, H. H. Richardson (great emotionalist of the Romanesque revival) was the one whose influence the master most felt. And John Root, another fertile rival of that time who knew less than the master but felt almost as much. The master admitted he sometimes shot very straight indeed. They were his only peers. And they were only feeling their way. But he was thinking *and* feeling—far in advance of either—to the new.

The Auditorium Building is largely what it is, physically, owing to Dankmar Adler's good judgment and restraining influence. It was Louis Sullivan who made it sing; made it music for Music.

The Getty Tomb in Graceland Cemetery was entirely his own; fine sculpture. A statue. A great poem addressed to human sensibilities as such. Outside the realm of music what finer requiem?

But—when he brought the drawing board with the motive for the Wainwright outlined in profile and elevation upon it and threw the board down on my table I was perfectly aware of what had happened.

This was a great Louis H. Sullivan moment. The tall building was born tall. His greatest effort? No. But here was the "skyscraper": a new thing beneath the sun, entity imperfect, but with virtue, individuality, beauty all its own. Until Louis Sullivan showed the way, high buildings lacked unity. They were built-up in layers. All were fighting height instead of gracefully and honestly accepting it. What unity those false masonry masses have that now pile up toward big-city skies is due to the master mind that first perceived the high building as a harmonious unit—its height triumphant.

The Wainwright Building was *tall*. It prophesied the way for these tall office-building effects we now point to with pride. And so to this day the Wainwright remains the master key to the "skyscraper" so far as "skyscraper" is a matter of architecture.

Only the golden interior of the Chicago Auditorium, the golden doorway of the purely pictorial Transportation Building (for what it is worth), the Getty Tomb, and the Wainwright Building are necessary to show the great reach of creative activity that was Louis Sullivan's. Other buildings the firm did, but all were more or less on these stems. Some were grafted upon these, some were grown from alongside them. But all were relatively inferior in point of the quality which we finally associate with the primitive strength of the thing that got itself born regardless, *true* to the idea.

The capacity for love—ardent, true, poetic—was great in him as his system of ornament, alone—with no buildings—proves. Say this greatest feature of his work was esoteric. Is it the less precious for that?

Do you realize that here, in his own way, is no body of culture evolving through centuries of time but a scheme and "style" of plastic expression which an individual, working away in the poetry-crushing environment of a more cruel materialism than any seen since the days of the brutal Romans, had made out of himself? Here was a sentient individual who evoked the goddess whole civilizations strove in vain for centuries to win, and wooed her with this charming interior smile—all on his own in one lifetime all too brief.

Regarding his achievement we may see the time coming when every man may have that precious quality called style for his very own.

Ah, that supreme erotic adventure of the mind that was his fascinating ornament!

Genius the master had, or rather, genius had him. Genius possessed him. It reveled in him and squandered him because he squandered genius.

The effect of any genius is seldom seen in his own time. Nor can the full effects of genius ever be traced or seen. Human affairs are continually flowing. What we call Life is, in everything eventful—plastic. It is a becoming and is so in spite of all efforts to fix it with names; all endeavors to make it static to man's will. As a pebble cast into the ocean sets up reactions lost in the faint encircling ripples of vast distances of eternity so does a man's genius go on forever. For genius *is but an expression of* principle. Therefore in no way does genius ever run counter to genius nor ever could. It is itself a human *element:* Nature.

We may be sure that the intuitions and expressions of such a nature as his in any work to which he lovingly put his hand is more conservative of the future where architecture of our country is concerned than all the schools of all time ever were even when combined with all the salesmanship of all the functioneers everywhere.

Now long ago, weak, weary, in a despondent moment not long before he died, he said to me, "Frank, our people have stopped thinking! It would be harder now to do radical work and more difficult to get radical work accepted than it ever was."

The drift toward mediocrity, taking the name of democracy in vain, had already set in. I see it now myself. It seems inevitable? No! great master. There is no such "inevitable." There is never an "inevitable" contrary to the life of the human soul—the life of love. The torch flung to your master hand from depths of antiquity kept alight and held aloft by you as long as you could breathe, shall not go out! It has ever been flung from hand to hand—since time began for man. Never yet have men been able to put it out!

CHAPTER SIX

THE UNITARIAN ABSTRACT: THE MODERN ESSENCE

Against threatening forces of Nature and the merciless passions of our fellow men, only a cultivated sense of organic form can build for democratic man an appropriate state, a deeper—therefore stronger—culture than mankind has yet known.

But observe how little of ORGANIC FORM is yet seen in our civilization! The cold abstractions of Western philosophy, scholastic materialism, the degenerate, because expedient, religions of our immediate world. All these have attributed the innate affirmations of the individual soul to the mysticism of a pseudo-romantic order! But modern thought is rapidly shifting. The old center-line, Romance, is to be found now in organic search for the organic reality that is poetic. And poetic is organic. This shift in the center-line of our utmost thought in philosophy or architecture (they now go together) comes in time to shame the expediency of our sham civilization for the lack of any culture at all. The one word necessary to deal with reality is the word *organic*—but like the word Nature it is the word least understood of any root-word in English. The deeper significance of the word is least known where the dictum, "a house is a machine for living," lies in ambush; there where the disparate fascist nature of our body-politic is becoming more evident. As the new source of physical power comes in a military uniform instead of overalls to supplant or supplement the old order, we may look for the end of all freedom: subjection of all men to standardization as themselves a kind of machinery.

FORM AND IDEA ARE INSEPARABLE

The cult of the unitarian abstraction is now salvation. But if divorced from realities it, too, is bound to produce failures, so let us turn the dogma—"Form Follows Function"—inward. Use both the word organic and the word Nature in deeper sense—essence instead of fact: say *form and function are one*. Form and idea then do become inseparable; the consequence not material at all except as spiritual and material are naturally *of* each other. Organic architecture does prove the unity of structure and the unity of the nature of aesthetics with principle. Instead of an aesthetician we have a constructor worthy to be an architect. It is in the new reality we now call romance to believe they become so.

But if form and idea are really one almost all the architectures of our known world would wither to be—so far as the life of today is concerned—topical makeshifts. Because glass and steel and the machine, until today, were unknown. So rare are the exceptions that we will find no buildings to imitate! The now "classic" architecture of ancient Greece or any fruit of the Greeks' successful search for the elegant solution is especially useless to us. Their aesthetic search gave us the vase as an objective complete in itself—now "classic"; gave us real sculpture and was the model of what we call "classic architecture." Both vase and sculpture were not too regardful of the nature of environment and their buildings were built by the chattel slave for a more concentrated slavery—that of the mind. In our hands, both became more and more oblivious of any use, oblivious to the nature of materials and to men as man.

THE PRISON HOUSE FOR THE MIND

In the new light of "use" as a basis for ORGANIC FORM we must find Grecian building to be without organic sense, ignorant of the nature of materials and careless of the Nature of humane purpose. Greece was wholly ignorant of organic principle in conceiving a building. The Greeks painted everything they produced as architecture, regardless of the beauty of materials used, and to them buildings were only a kind of sculpture more and more fashioned from outside inward. Intellectual? They were. But the question now arises why should we with a deeper philosophy of our own use their abstractions (coming over to us by way of such utter disciples, such grafts, as the Paris Beaux Arts, Oxford, Harvard, or Yale)—all boulevards. These new-world disciples of old-world slavery make a virtue of trying to live, build, and shine by imitation; sowing distrust of originality. Disciples we all are to some degree. It is hard to be an honorable one either way—good or bad. But in this affair with the Greeks we do reveal our inferiority complex as a bad (dishonest) disciple if we mean to build for democracy.

Well . . . this pseudo-search of the Greeks for the elegant imposition rather than a search for the more natural solution—preferably the exception that proves the rule—dazzled and demoralized us while these ideals of organic architecture were yet either absent or too novel. The nature of organic character as a matter of the third dimension is still scarcely understood. Greek culture (as were most of the great antique cultures) was imbued by imposing sense of the complete altogether. By rationalizing superficiality they reduced architecture to a science but did not evolve a building as great art. If—as we are now using the word *Nature* in interior sense—we were once to apprehend the lack of this inward *Nature* of their thought where building is the concern, and therefore become able to see the superficial character of Oxfordian-Greek abstractions, therefore the structures derived from them to form the basis of our education; we would regard imitation of the Greeks as voluntarily going to prison. Prison because, excepting primitive Dorian temples honestly built in wood, the "modern" Greeks were incapable of free—that is to say, true—building. Their later stone (marble) structures were all false structures by way of imitations of early wood temples. The stone itself—a beautiful translucence in that climate—was completely painted. They painted everything, regardless of materials. Even their life itself became an elegant form of painted sculpture. In many respects very beautiful sculpture. Yes, but based upon no truly spiritual life concept. Theirs was a civilization that died because it was Grecian to live upon elegance as a substitute for soul. Greek philosophy did contribute to modern discipleship the intellectual abstraction which Plato saw as "the eternal idea of the thing." But their own "idea" of the thing was as viewed from outside. Their splendidly sculptural externality became "the glory that was Greece," therefore "the grandeur that was Rome." As a consequence, Greek culture became the aim or pretense of all subsequent monarchic rule and empire. So, stately Greece—exquisite as a statue—was inevitable parent of the degenerate *ism*, the consequent *ist*, and ever present *ite* to which we have dedicated the intellectual life of our nation in our universities. Thomas Jefferson is thus memorialized; Abraham Lincoln so entombed; our best minds falsely prisoned or ignored by the modern temples of universal knowledge.

No—there could be nothing in the culture of incestuous Greece or bloody Rome to inspire organic structure in building, statesmanship, or philosophy—or for a culture true to democracy in the realm of aesthetics, the realm of ethics, or religion. Unless our attempt to propagate a culture of our own is vain we cannot follow the Greeks until we understand them better than we do.

Should our democracy now determine to build for the freedom peculiar to itself, our ideology could well serve for the emancipation of humanity. I believe this nation *will* so build. Our cities will spread thin; our schools will become natural; our lives not reckoned in "freedoms" will be basically free; disciples will become more honest even though presumptive followers; and the apprentice will be a true workman with proper pride in the doing, loving to see that doing well done. To be able to work at and for what one most wants to do well should be gospel in our democracy. For a democratic slogan try "What a man does *that* he has."

Were we now to apprehend innate limitations of Greek culture that culture might become as useful to us as it has hindered us in this affair of mass-education and made (is still making) of the Greek abstraction a prison house for the mind. The freedom of the new romance? Well ... you *will not* find it in Grecian art or mythology. Find it inside the modern democratic man: "What a man does—*that* is his." His vitality as an individual is *his reality* in the new romance; his honor and therefore the basis for creation. Organic architecture comes with that romantic reality to you today. As a man is, so he must build. Just as a nation builds—so that nation is. We have the buildings we deserve to have either as men or as man. There are many ways in life to conceal a man's true nature but when he builds he cannot hide. You have him as he is.

Within these paragraphs concerning the Grecian myth you may find why democracy has, as yet, built nothing for itself?

CHAPTER SEVEN

MOBOCRACY AND GENIUS

Demoralization of the creative instinct—O Lord, be merciful—lies in this universified, governmentalized substitution of a falsely decorated *mobocracy* for the thought-built *democracy* we might have. This wretched graft of which we are inordinately proud has so blinded us that already it is difficult for us even to recognize the dishonesty from which we spring and in which we live, and from which we will have suffered the greatest of all losses in this passing era of the omnipresent borrower, arrant physicist, and this ismic salesman—the artist. It is he who is primarily to blame! The weakling has not been equal to his true place. He has been a coward when and wherever his people needed his vision and courage most. Throw him in with the professionals, journalists, and the art critic (with his camera) and for good measure throw in the "history of art" as usually taught. They all belong together. Of such sham are the implements by which we work our intolerable waste: the misuse or abuse of our bravest and best; the chronic substitution of quantity for quality; guesswork instead of interior discipline and no instruction in organic construction on a good foundation, all down the line! These add up to the ruin of the creative instinct of any nation. This defect is now either the entertainment or the popular punishment meted out to the fire-born by our false success-ideal. By odious comparison genius is today just about where Louis H. Sullivan was yesterday; the life of the human spirit is wasted more securely than ever: waste sustained by authority for our already enormously increasing masses of "ownership." Even as in that day the stronger the property habit in the life of the masses—the more our bias is totalitarian. Ownership unless unusually natural and enlightened does not tend democratic. Our young men are not urged, they are hunger-driven by false standards of success toward standardization, first, and ideas based on principle—if any—afterward. *To oppose this trend toward makeshift lives more and more standardized* is where we find the same old human frontier upon which organic architecture as great art must now go to work. Science—as inspiration—is through. In any long view science cannot substitute for Nature. It may take Nature apart but cannot put Nature together again for the growth of the human soul.

A dense conspiracy of the matter-of-fact against the human spirit is what monitors this science mentality we are calling a civilization—one which science has presented and promoted. Meantime we are miscalling our confused art and sterilized education "culture" when both destroyed by science are mainly tools for money-making. Invention? Only another tool for the same purpose. As a matter of course, such "art," "education," and "invention" allow us no fundamental architecture of our own. How, then, can democracy build? We have brains enough. We have the tools. But we have no true mind at this crucial moment in this matter of the structure of a native architecture natural to us. An affair of genuine culture, it lies far beyond the cowardly revival of the classics versus the two-dimensional patterns of the "modernist" and we have little deep conviction concerning the reality of anything if *we can't see* it work by being taught to see only in the "flat"; spiritual integrity—*depth*—always the unwelcome intruder. We do not dare to think for fear we might feel our insignificance? We are afraid to feel for fear of our thought otherwise. Nor have we deep enough faith in ourselves as ourselves to realize that the basis of democracy is—teaching men, or allowing them "to know themselves." No. Wherever the deeper essentials of life are concerned, we are craven cowards. A rat-like perspicacity? We have it, and the same courage.

It has always been difficult for me to see the grandeur of promiscuity. The horse there, too, is behind the cart. Honor hides behind the barn.

But at least so long as we are not yet committed to the mobocrat's idea of "the common man" there is hope. I have never yet met this "common man." In a democracy it is you and it is I who are the protagonists of any future that is now—democratic or fascist. And that means no future for us as a democratic nation is to be found by condoning imitations by disciples, to live in, or in sending youth to standardized schools; perfectly good plums to get back prunes.

THE SENSE OF GUILT

Now, to say that the ideal disciple—man or nation—is hard to find may of course be only a way of saying that the ideal master does not exist?

Somehow I've always felt that were the master ideal his disciple would be so—even if in spite of himself. Does the disciple not reflect the master and exaggerate his mortality just as he does his immortality?

Did not Judas personify these forces? Probably he did.

Is there no ideal discipleship because the relationship is wrong? Is it all too human to be ideal discipline for the son of a technocracy without soul so far going, going, gone from democracy as this one of ours? To look to *any* disciple for *his own integrity* due to experience by interior discipline? Is this like looking for light in a place inevitably in the dark shadow of false eminence? But if not false, why dark; eminence should be luminous? Why is it not so for the youths of our modern world? Is it because we continue to propagate them and murder them by conscription, vast mass-education, and bad politics? Where does the faith of the neophyte lie now? I don't know . . . of course, the mechanical pace is fast; competition in this and that, meum and tuum, is more and more keen. The higher the education, the more grossly expedient it is. Life by imitation like a sickness spreads wide and thin over the vast surface of a continent. Government is becoming enormity, mostly burdensome bureaucratic expropriation, punishment, or propaganda for the business of war and the preservation of the "to-have-and-to-hold" we call "security." Such intensity as we know is mostly the voracity we call speed and the desperation we call "efficiency." Both are objectionable just as light on a purposely hidden crime would be.

But I do know by the flippant attitudes of arrant, national egotism that nobility of spirit is condemned to die by unimaginative reason or worse—the arrogant humility of our very best people. In what we call production and success there is no longer the spirit of youth because there is no firm platform nor any springboard at all for truly creative imagination. In this civilization, premature by way of science and sudden riches—probably proceeding from barbarism to degeneracy with stunning waste of power—genius is a sin against the mob! It is the calamity of our time that no master, were he to come to us today, could survive to enjoy true, that is to say, secure fame. Notoriety—no end—would be all he could hope for during his lifetime. If any post-mortem "halo" for him, dead, it would have to be carefully adjusted, by experts, to shed agreeable light on the establishments endorsed by the canonizers themselves. Their name is legion.

Something very like this massacre upon the life of imaginative reason, an assassination of which I write with unsympathetic patience and moderated invective, lieber-meister had many times more bitterly described to me. Some day some other original, wishful lover of a liberal architecture for the coming of age of our democracy, will be writing of it all as happening to him.

In due course when some *qualified* historian—a barbarian perhaps now that we hoard and hide the atom bomb—may refer to the architecture of the late nineteenth and early twentieth centuries, what honor it has will be found so far as the life of architecture is new—not renewed—to stem directly from one Louis H. Sullivan of Adler and Sullivan, Architects, Chicago, Illinois, say, in the late eighteen-nineties?

As a matter of course, only the higher discipleship which it is fair to say education is could have missed the master's own good book, "The Autobiography of an

Idea"? I find many high-school boys have read it, also the Mayor of Louisville, Kentucky. His name is Farnsley.

Now, as for my place in the practice of that idea—with my inside eyes wide-open I chose to go with Louis H. Sullivan at the proper time to be "the pencil in his hand." Later I left him to carry on my work in my way as I best could. I came back to him as an architect and a friend about twenty years later, not long enough before he dropped by the wayside. Leaving that wayside with contempt, but hope, I have persistently worked. I remember the master once saying to me, sadly (he was writing something about the apparently miraculous survival of the Imperial Hotel in the Tokio temblor of 1922): "Frank, you have never been my disciple—but you are the only one who ever worked with me who understood. I couldn't do what you've done, nor could you have done what you've done but for me!"

What did the master mean? He meant that though inspired by him I had not copied his work. I have never imitated him or anyone. He was great enough to be proud of me because I wasn't his disciple. He had no more respect for disciples than for a draughtsman.

I am proud to have worked by his side inspired to this day by him. A master! Yes. But no more mine than yours or anyone's who will *understand* what he understood and be faithful to that comprehension. This entire aftermath we call history, and are taught to teach to teachers to teach, must have been mis-made in some such equivocal fashion as I have seen history made of his work and my own in architecture. More hapless "text" mis-made to be mis-read. I have seen the whole "movement" since inception trickle in little by little, the mere "look-of-the-thing" meantime so manipulated as to confuse and confound the simple truth because to some unqualified but all the more presumptuous writer it seemed unpleasant, or expedient, to disagree. I have seen the long arm of co-incidence manipulated to reflect borrowed credit where it could not belong—and lived to see this expedient remouthed as prejudiced propaganda. Pretentious or ignorant personalities writing in the name of art in all nations have taken a fling at the subject, all professing advanced perspective from bad matter-of-fact or none. I have seen this "civilization" of ours itself excel in such conscienceless equivocation and by way of unlimited exercises of equivocal character become unanimously exterior, quite satisfied to be merely careerist. More shameless evasion or shallow pretense characterizes the phase of our mentality we call "art" than any I know—but perhaps only because I have seen this phase of our disgrace grow up.

Sophisticates obsessed by the notion that culture with a capital C for our lives must come from "abroad," play upon this weakness of ours. The exhibitionist criticism of the museum seems unaware that most of the modernist movements it presents, imagining them good for a sensation, derive from monarchy and are consciously or unconsciously bound to the roots of fascism. A bitter smile from me—to see the "trend" wherever the driver spoke with suitable foreign accent. I have come to see for myself—finally—what the master himself said with extreme disgust (and unusual profanity): "Wright! . . . why are they [the American people] so g—— d—— credulous?" Many years later when he always called me "Frank" he would say wearily, "Frank, our people don't think any more." But let me here confess: imported endorsements are nearer the truth than our own authorities ever were on the subject. But if our own crop of disciples is without honor, what of the country itself that produces them in school, in art, in politics, in religion, "ad libitum ad nauseam"? Such a state would have to die not as Louis H. Sullivan died with honor, unsuccessful, alone, but dishonored in the mass by its own kind of "success."

Now, why all this attention to the specious disciple? For one thing, reflections from the master to whom I listened a half-century ago now verified by my own experience.

For another (maybe an attempt to unscramble eggs), on account of the way I have seen history "scrambled" by disciples and come down the line deformed in respect to Louis H. Sullivan, myself, and the new architecture. In books, pamphlets, magazines, newspapers, and in all languages it has come until all history—for me—assumes a spurious aspect. With complete skepticism I now read whatever is written not only on the new architecture but any other subject. I want to know "written by whom," then "what about the writer"? When I feel I know the thing as pretentious or the usual posterior-personal slant, I throw the equivocal mass away and try to form an opinion from between the lines. I suggest that you, kind reader, do the same here. No self-portrait or portrayal of one person by another nor any report of a cause however great or small—or of both put together—as is the case here—can be impersonal. Nor should be. As for fame—fame will always mean more to posterity than it can ever mean to the recipient alive or dead. Thought by callow youth to be fun—to the famous man fame is likely to be only funny.

CONCERNING THE APPRENTICE

Now that we have looked this gift horse, the disciple, in the mouth—the apprentice! What about the volunteer apprentice? It is my feeling and experience that the volunteer apprentice is a better basis for a future architecture for democracy than the selective disciple. Probably the only way we will achieve a great architecture. We can make best use of our best youth that way. The apprentice comes next to the doing of the thing to put his hand to it. What quality he has is soon put to test. He makes good or he loses out. As he is situated, next to spirit, character counts most. He has a chance to develop kindness, understanding, encouragement, and companionship by way of sacrifice to his ideal. Pretense is vain. Presumption is upset. By his performance he is known, and the shirker is soon shown up by the worker. In quality the apprentice is likely to remain fresh and honest because he shares by his own ability in creative effort of unquestioned superiority or else he would be no voluntary apprentice.

A GOOD APPRENTICE IS ABLE TO SERVE WITHOUT BECOMING A VASSAL

As distinguished from the disciple the apprentice confronts his preference and is in position to serve reality. But he may become a disciple, lose contact with his conscience, and so lower his character in selfish pursuit of his own consequence at expense to his art.

But as a creative force his chance of survival in his chosen field is far greater than any chance due the ambiguous disciple. There may be infinite disciples but comparatively few apprentices. The psychology of the modern apprentice therefore differs radically from that of the disciple although the apprentice may become a disciple, deceive himself, and disintegrate. To the apprentice belongs the responsible, direct approach; the approach of the disciple is intuitive, mainly selfish, and irresponsible. The apprentice works with direct responsibility to and for his inspiration. The disciple presumes upon whatever relationship he has to the master. Of the two—the apprentice has foundation in actual service to his ideal. The disciple has at best assumed elevation without any sacrificial foundation. He has tried to take the short-cut. Hence the apprentice will realize what the disciple may only surmise. Withal the apprentice is straightforward, proceeding by experience from Nature to ethics and back again to the drawing board. The disciple is equivocal and knows no ethics. If and when both are men these comparisons are fair enough. The disciple has already sold his exemplar to his client in his own name. The apprentice will not so sell until he becomes a disciple. He would lose his credit and so his self-respect. To license him to build eventually would build up a profession being torn down now by favored sons with paper degrees.

The apprentice in a democracy does not differ so much from the apprentice of "*le moyen age*," except that, instead of the slave he then was, he is the comrade of his master, and to any extent he is able to live up to.

To detach oneself from the nature of the doing is the greatest calamity that can befall an apprentice. But the apprentice also is "loaded." The man who takes one is either brave or an incorrigible egoist. But his duty is clear. He must share himself with those who admire and trust him.

At the height of his power I knew Louis H. Sullivan—Master—as his right-hand man. And it is in the nature of what I have said that all I could honestly tell of him is personal to me. I can give the master to you only by way of his draughtsman, myself. Inasmuch as you can only see him here through me, if intimately of him this "writing" is inevitably intimate of me. So you know him by way of this willing pencil in his hand for nearly seven years. Who, then, was this Louis H. Sullivan I still call lieber-meister so long after he is gone because he is still an inspiration to me? How did this "pencil" come to his hand? This book is my attempt to answer.

From me at this time the first-person singular will offend many, surprise some, and disappoint more. But in this whole matter, at risk of rousing resentment among skeptical or unwilling readers (becoming myself liable to the charge of bad "taste" by hurting the feelings of others), wherever lieber-meister is concerned with me or I with him I have repeated complimentary or condemnatory words, both, as I well remember them. Because while this work is authentic it is no documentary treatise. I prefer the humble arrogance of sincerity to the arrogant humility of self-deception; so hypercriticism averse to the first-person singular would better not try to read it. I am more concerned with truth than fact. But when I use a fact the fact is fact.

This book is "in memoriam" because of a promise.

I do not like to write it because—but for the promise—it should be unnecessary to do so. Louis H. Sullivan—lyric poet—no functionalist—should, by now, be well known and cherished *for what his gift truly was;* his "gift" at the same time so much more (and other) than is on the record.

The profound naturalness of one's own being is the essential condition of a great architect, and the condition of greatness in the man. It has been the ambition of my life to achieve it with glass and steel—bricks, boards, a hod of mortar, a "client," and "the union."

So, wherever the practice of architecture today rises to the dignity of an idea in harmony with place and time, independent of ism, ist, or ite, the origin of that practice is middle-West to our courageous national experiment in freedom and stems from one, Louis H. Sullivan—beginning about 1889. But the pen is a tricky tool—fascinating but treacherous.

THE DRAWINGS

SELECTIONS FROM A SERIES OF ORIGINAL DRAWINGS BY THE MASTER, LOUIS
H. SULLIVAN, PRESENTED BY HIM TO FRANK LLOYD WRIGHT ON APRIL 11, 1924

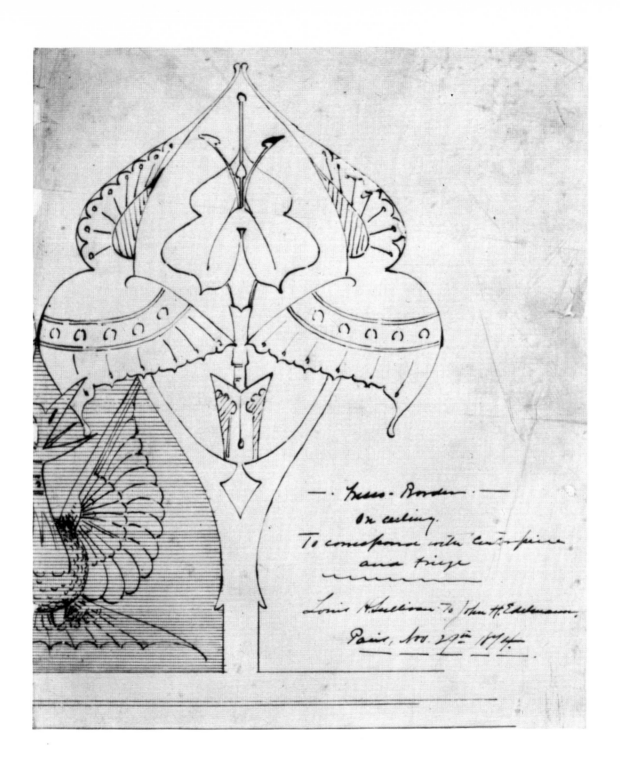

Early exercise at the Beaux Arts. Dedicated to John Edelman. Paris. 1875-80   **115**

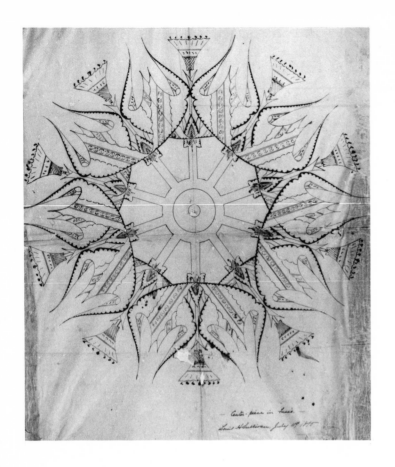

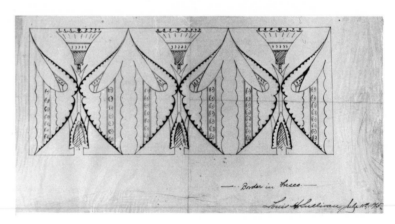

116   Beaux Arts exercises. Fresco patterns. Paris. 1875

Early Adler buildings. Terra cotta. Drafting for D. Adler and Company. Chicago, 1880   **117**

118   Boxes for the first McVicker's Theatre, Chicago. Painted wood and gilded plaster. Adler and Sullivan. 1884-85

Ornament detail. Gilded plaster.
First McVicker's Theatre. 1884-85

120   Plaster panel for first McVicker's Theatre. 1885

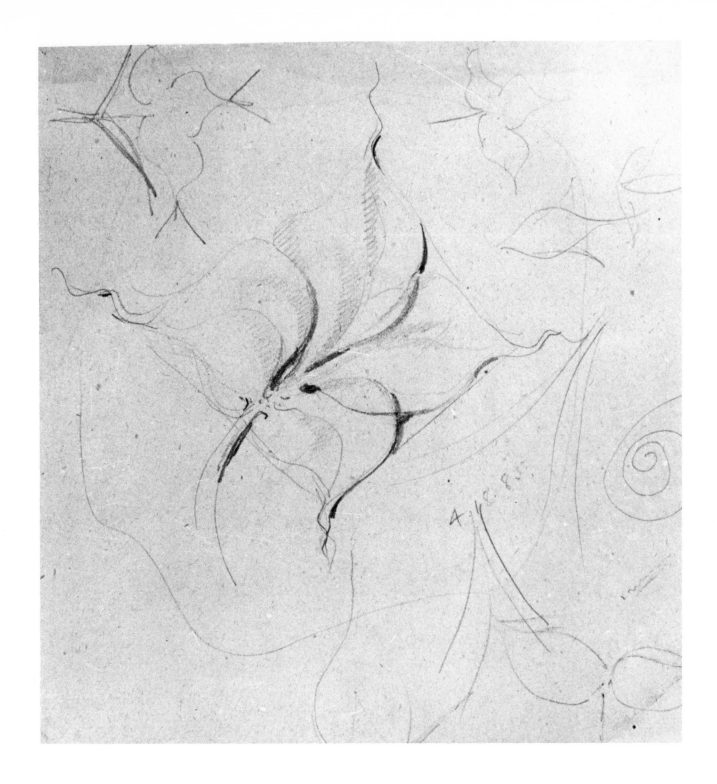

Study. Beginning of the plastic period. 1885-86   **121**

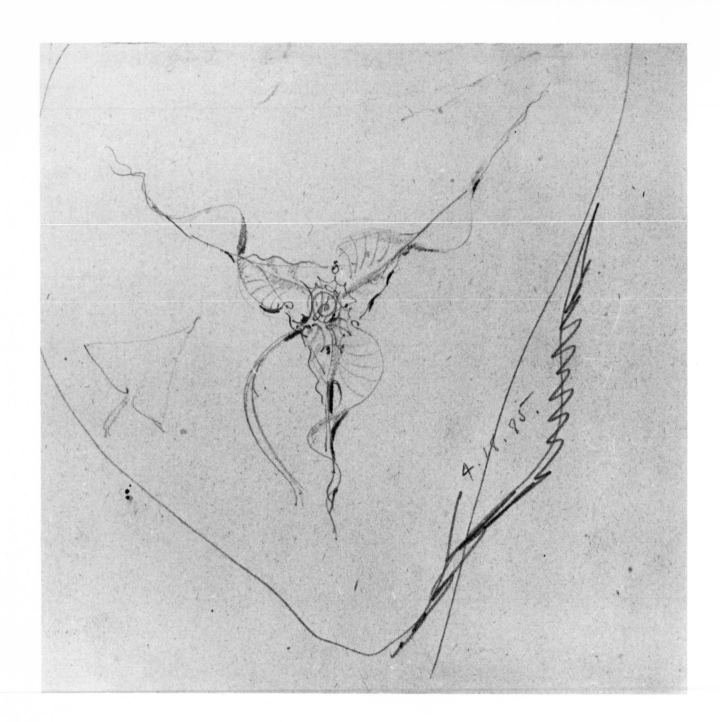

(This and facing page) Studies in plasticity. Terminology. Terra cotta. 1885

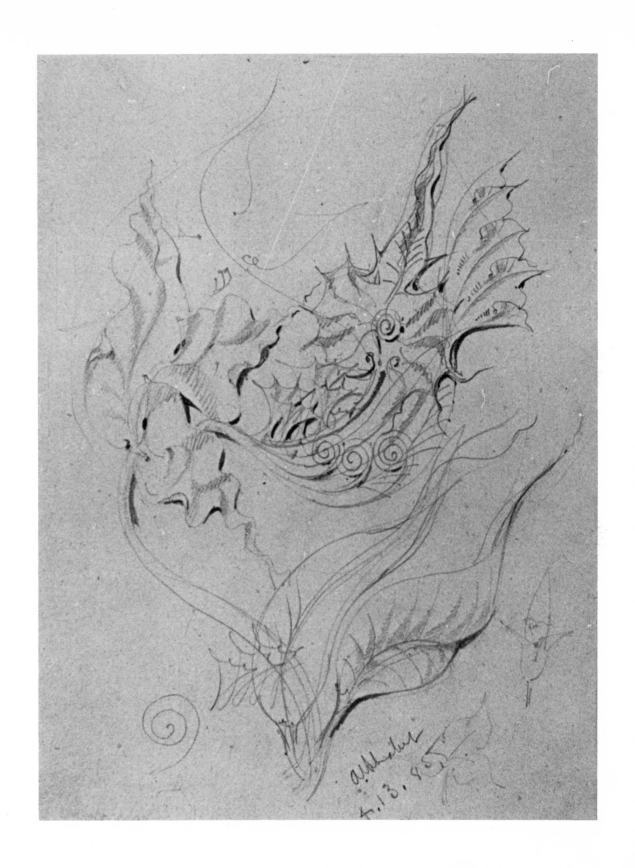

8.28.85

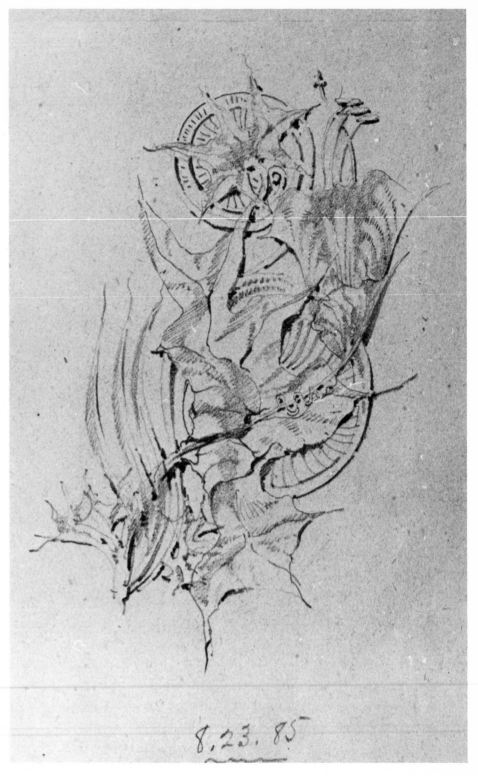

8.23.85

Studies in plasticity. Terra cotta. 1885

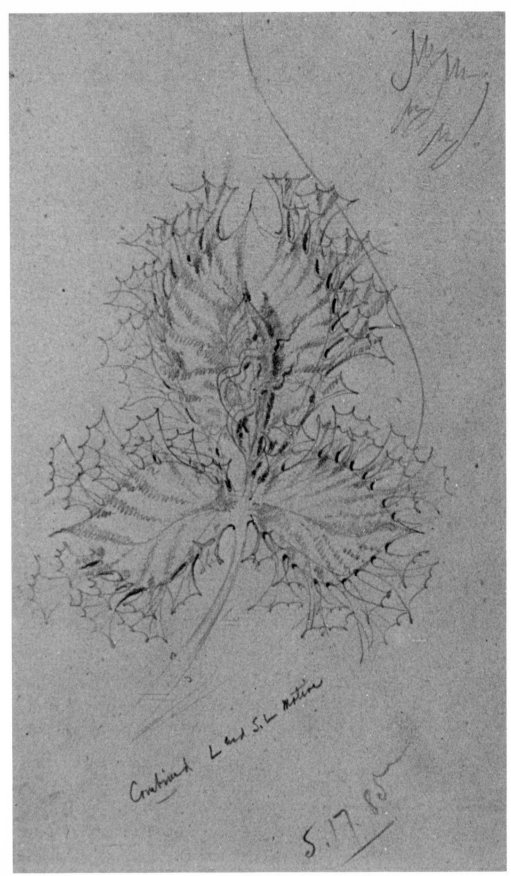

Study in differentiation. Terra cotta. 1885

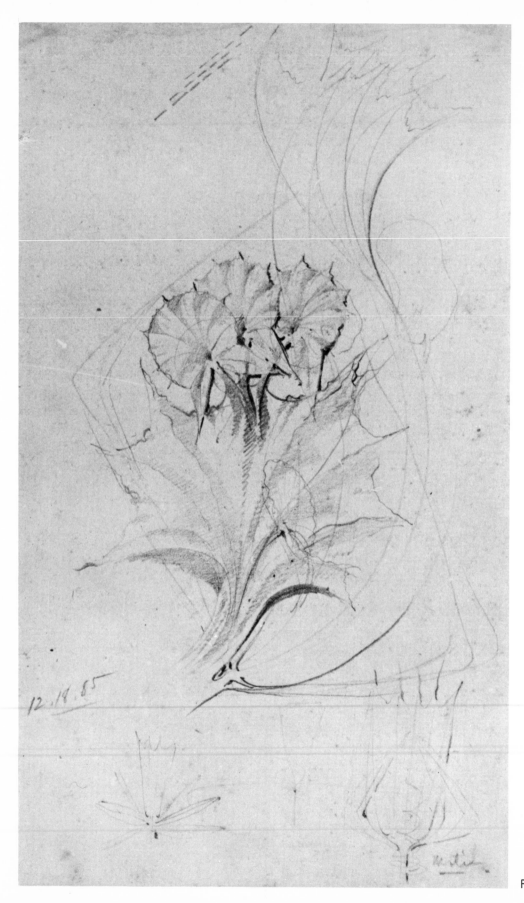

12.19.85

Plasticity. Study for terra cotta. 1885

Corbel for the Auditorium, Chicago. Plaster. 1887-88

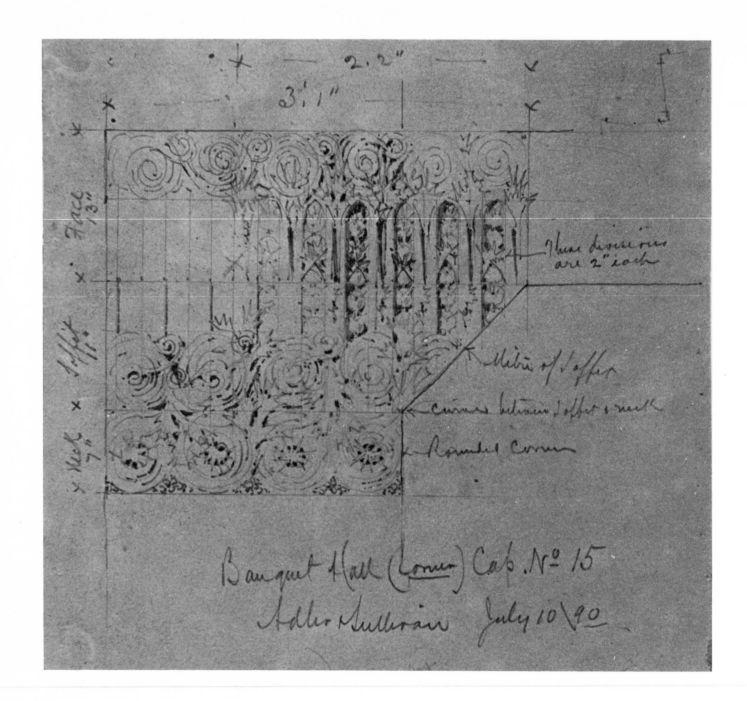

One of a series of fifteen carved wood capitals. Glued-up mahogany blocks. Auditorium banquet hall. 1890

One of the nine continuous plaster bands two feet wide on sounding board of proscenium. McVicker's Theatre rebuilt. 1890-91

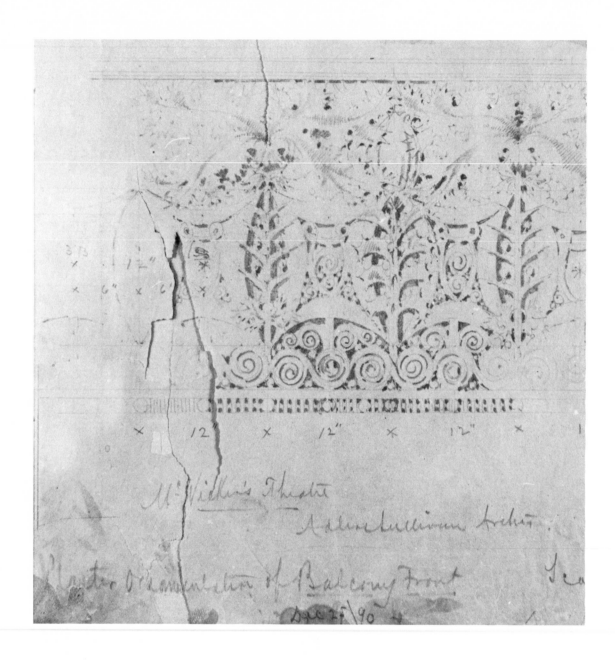

130   Balcony front. Plaster. Electric light set in ornament. McVicker's Theatre rebuilt. 1890

One of the nine plaster bands on sounding board
of proscenium. McVicker's Theatre rebuilt. 1890-91

One of the nine plaster bands on sounding board
of proscenium. McVicker's Theatre rebuilt. 1890-91

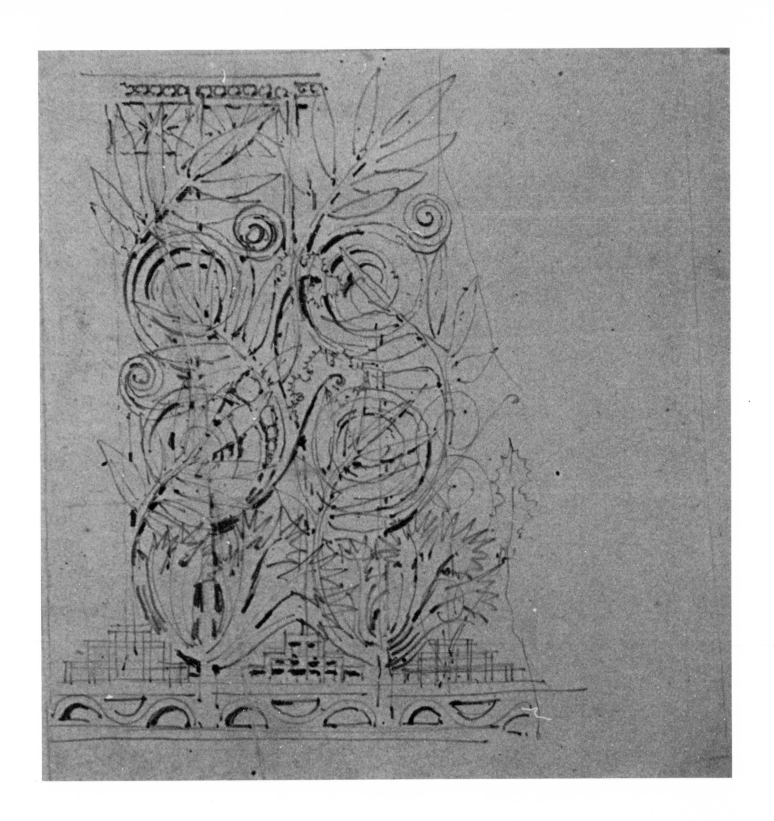

Frieze on foyer. Plaster. McVicker's Theatre rebuilt. 1891   **133**

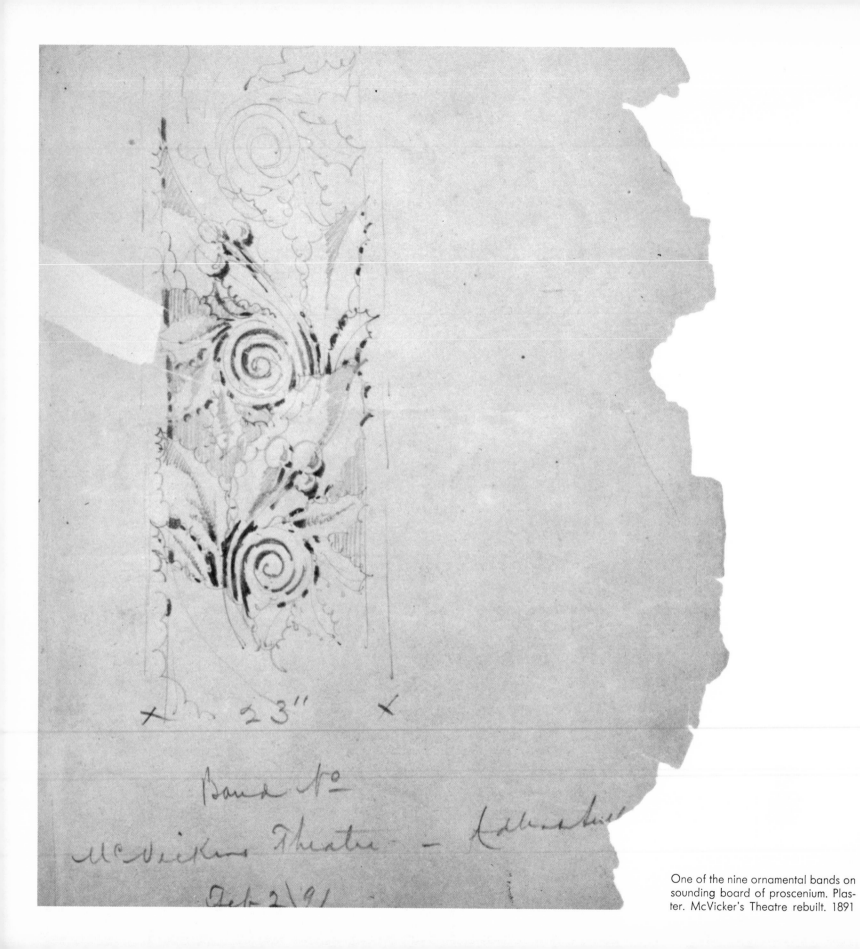

≈ 3"

Band N°

McVickers Theatre — Architecture

Feb 2\91

One of the nine ornamental bands on
sounding board of proscenium. Plaster. McVicker's Theatre rebuilt. 1891

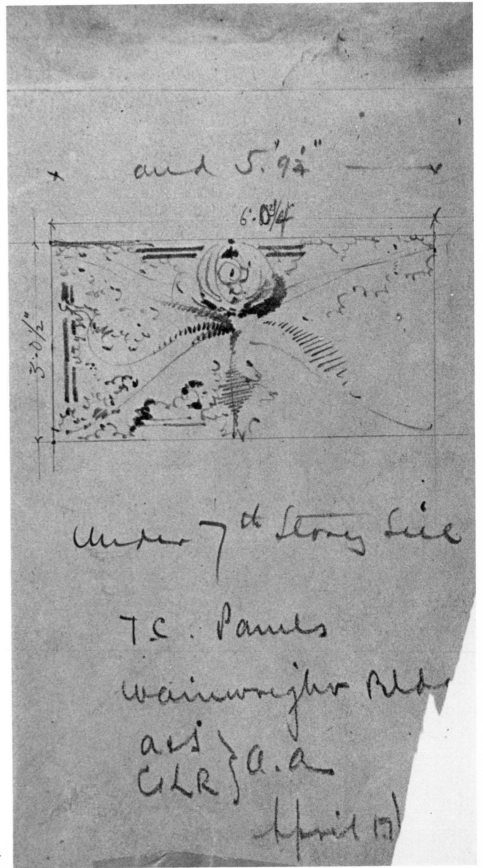

Terra cotta panel between windows.
Wainwright Building, Buffalo. 1891

Carving

Oct 16/90

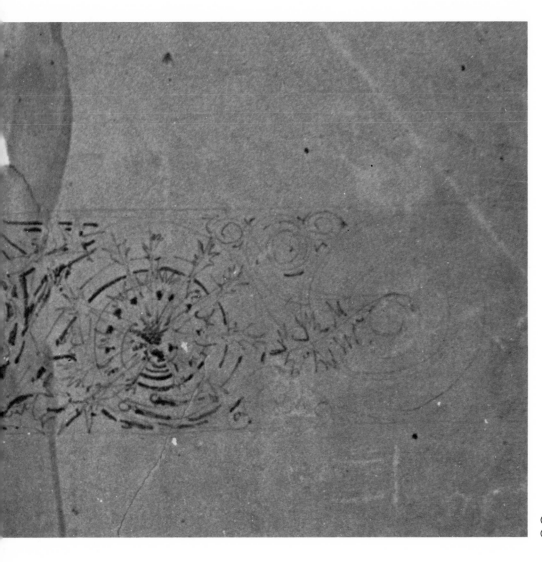

Carving of lower edge of granite arch, face and soffit.
Getty Tomb. Graceland Cemetery, Chicago. 1890-91

(Overleaf) Full size detail of stone carving of face and soffit of arch. Getty Tomb. 1890-91 **137**

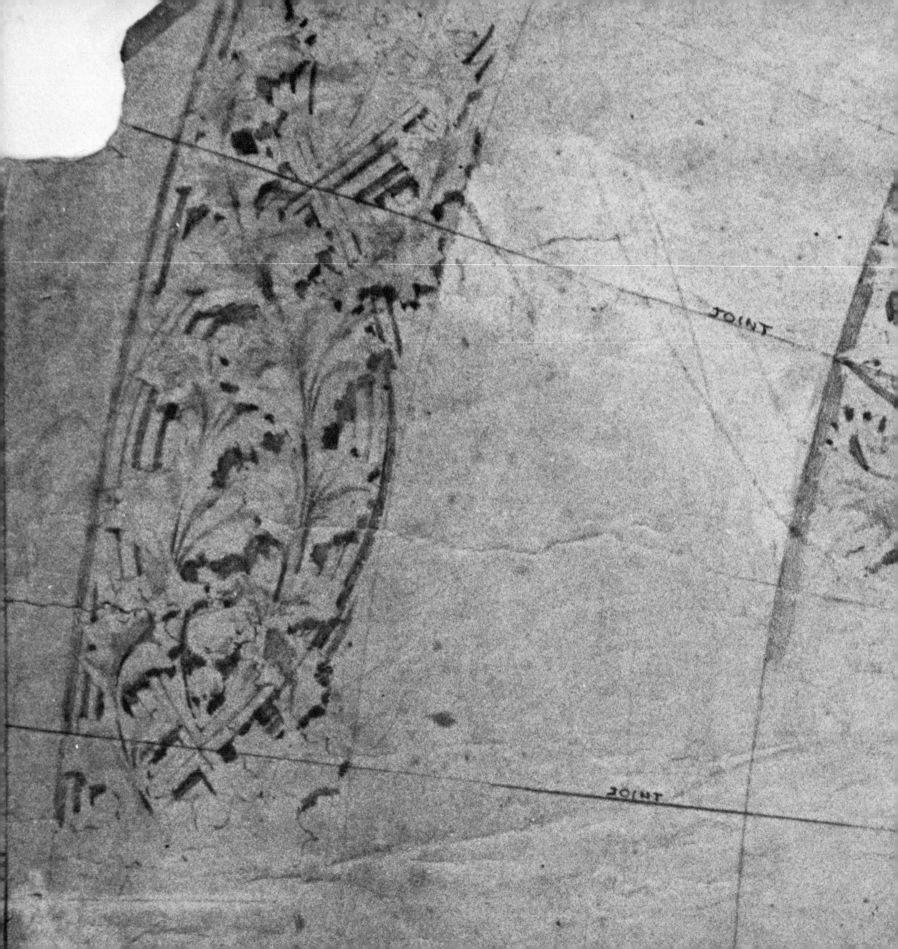

JOINT

JOINT

SOFFIT.

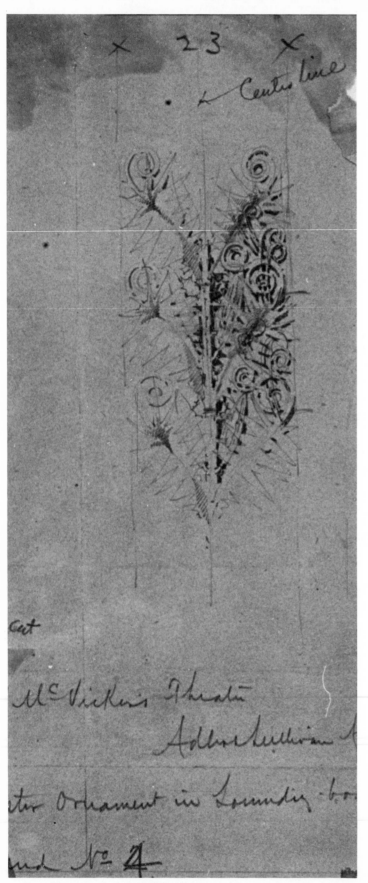

One of the nine ornamental bands on sounding board
of proscenium. Plaster. McVicker's Theatre rebuilt. 1891

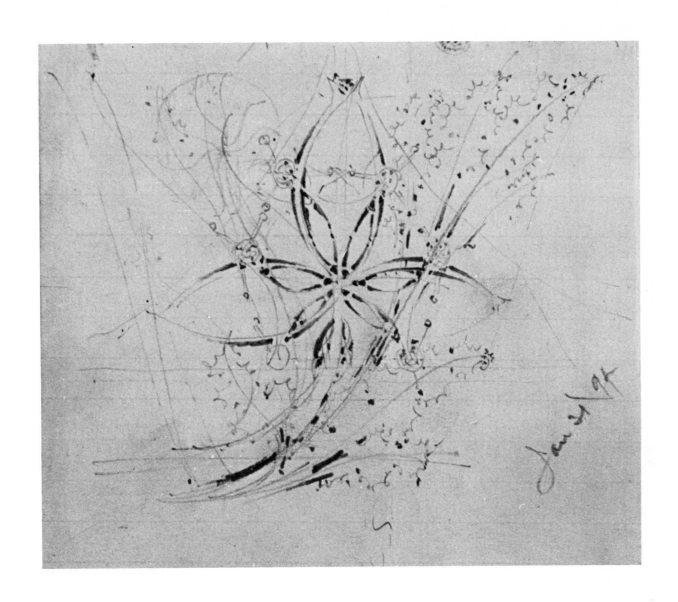

Study for terra cotta. 1894-95   **141**

2'.6"

X

(This and facing page)
Plaster soffits. Transportation Building, Chicago World's Fair. 1892-93

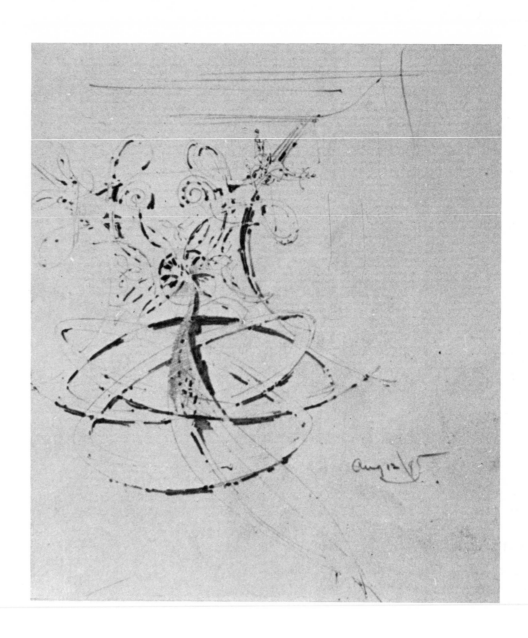

Study for terra cotta. 1894-95

144   (Facing page) Column cap in terra cotta. St. Nicholas Hotel, St. Louis. 1893-94

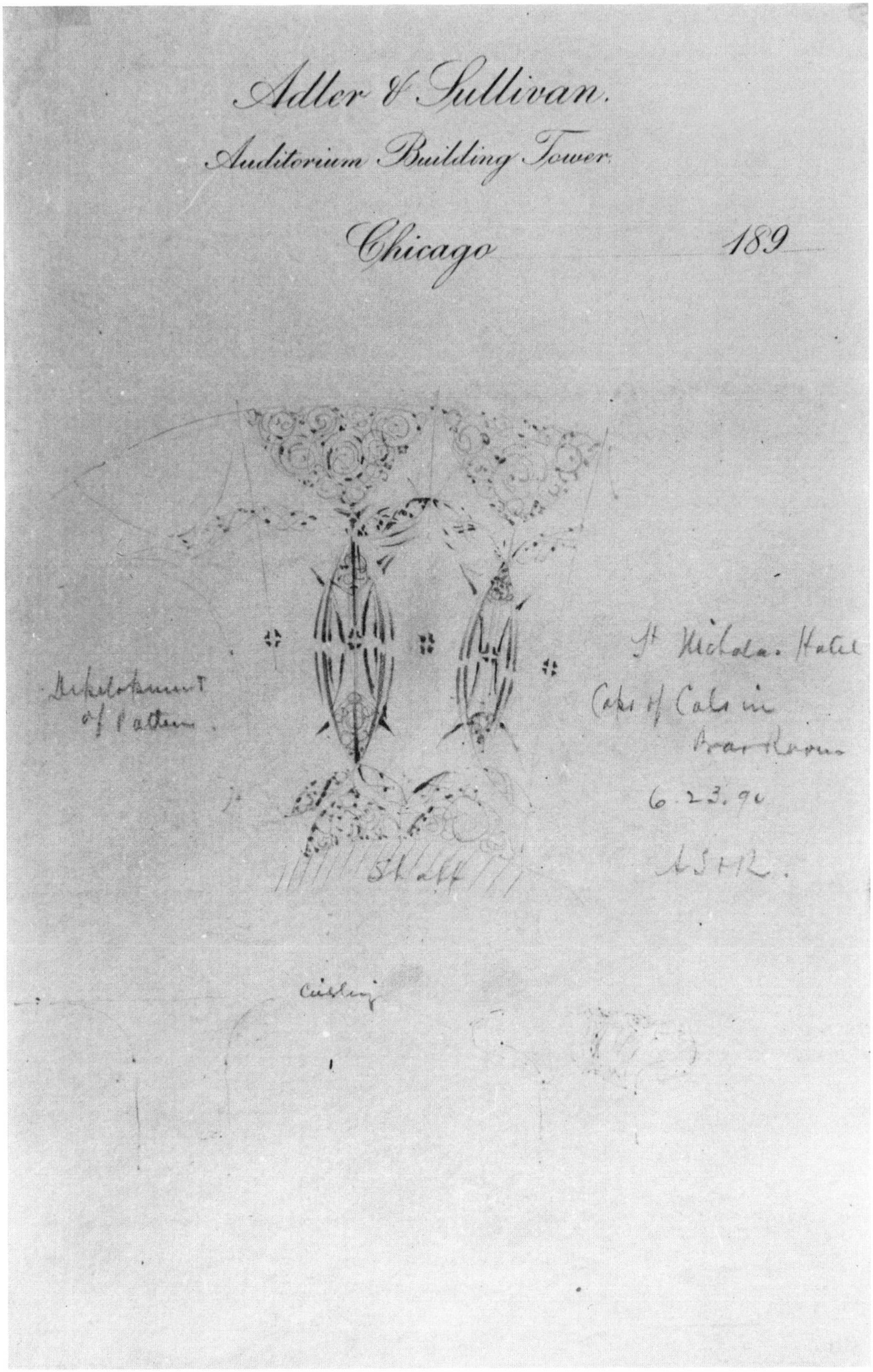

Adler & Sullivan.

Auditorium Building Tower.

Chicago   189

Development of Pattern.

St Nicholas Hotel
Cabs of Cabs in
Bear Room

6.23.90

ASM.

Shaft

Ceiling

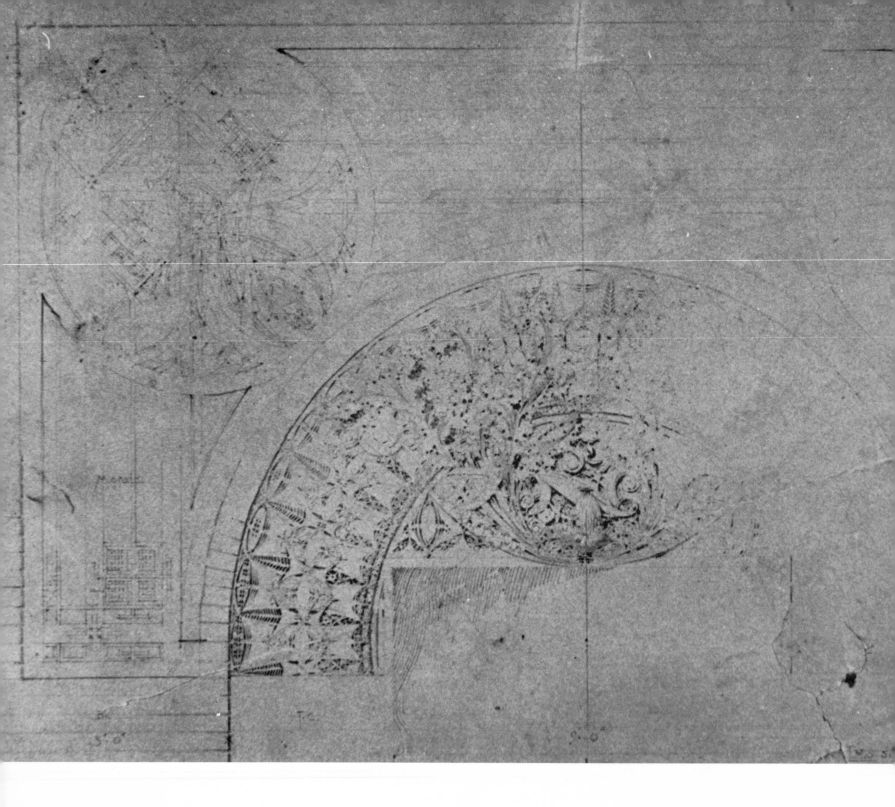

146   Brick and terra cotta fireplace. St. Nicholas Hotel, St. Louis. 1893-94

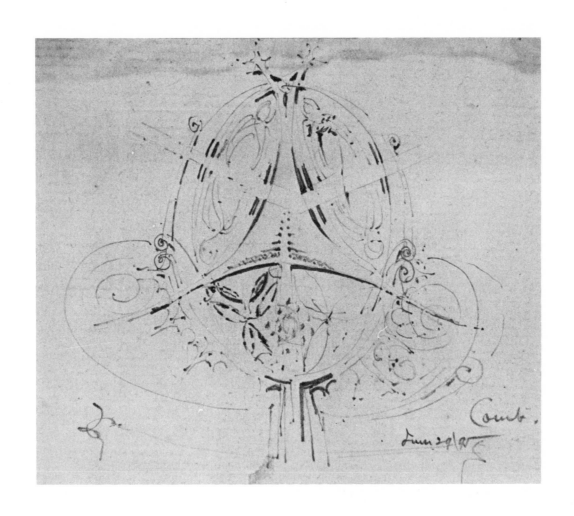

Carved amber comb. 1895   **147**

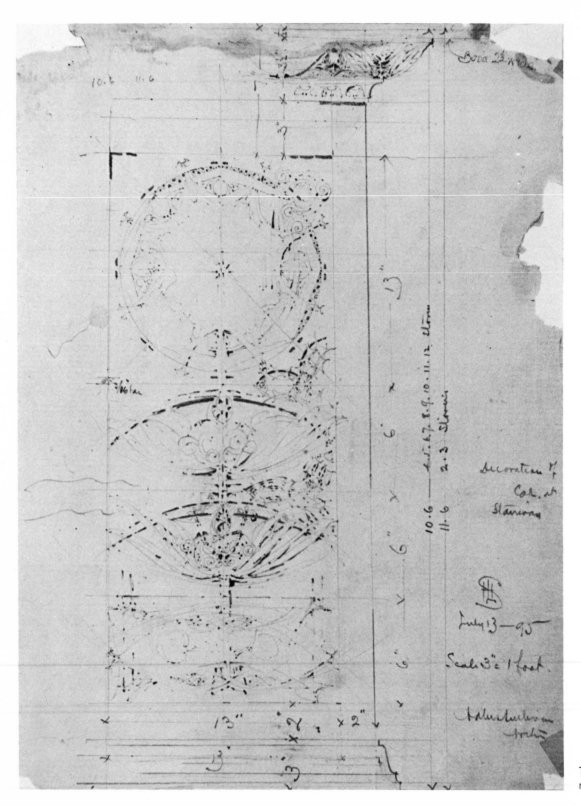

Terra cotta pier. Drawing shows change in method. Guaranty Building, Buffalo. 1895

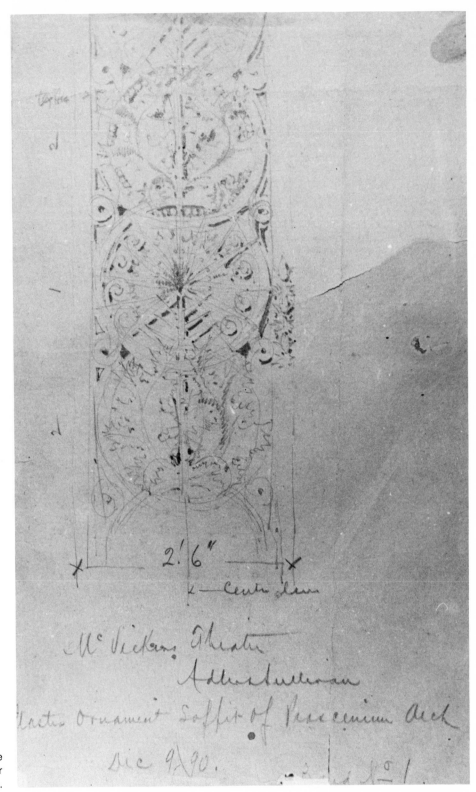

Similar design for second McVicker's Theatre dated 1890. Technique contrasting with later rendering of parallel drawing dated 1895.

Early studies at the Beaux Arts dated 1880.
Female figures from model.
Male figure after Michael Angelo.

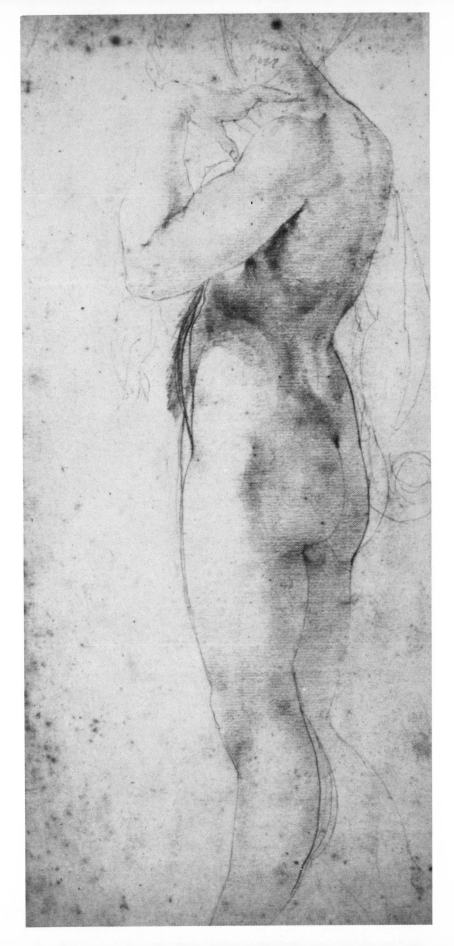

BOOK FOUR   PERSPECTIVE

If there be a poet possessed of knowledge without bias—an old Welshman free from perverseness—let him answer me.

—Taliesin, Bard of Britain

RETROSPECT

have only partly succeeded in doing what I would do if I could.

Not having so much to be humble about, I have tried—with honest arrogance—to describe the tragedy, triumph, and significance of the great man who invariably signed himself Louis H. Sullivan; to tell you why I, though never his disciple—nor that of any man—called him "lieber-meister." His own beautiful drawings, from which I have selected those you have seen used here, are better testimony than any I could offer in words. He had been dating the drawings (some wrongly but who really knows?) and as he put the collection of a hundred or more into my hands he said with a questioning look—I can see his glance as I write—"Frank, you will be writing about these some day?"

"Yes, lieber-meister, I will."

And I remember that, in his weakness, he seemed relieved and pleased. These drawings were the dearest treasure of his heart and this book is the true story of a personal experience now necessary to put on the record, no more for his sake than for my own, because the historical view of each where the other is concerned is getting so badly out of focus that only I can right it. I meant to write not *as* the disciple I never was, nor the pupil he never wanted, but write as the capable workman who understood (that is to say, loved) the man he served—a man who loved him in return. From me should come appreciation of the master's work as the master himself saw his own work and as I saw him. But this book is not about him—it is about our work-life and struggle while we were together

True appreciation of his contribution if not of his true quality goes further and further astray both ways. This is partly owing to the blind-spots inevitable to badly conceived history but somewhat more to a tribe of imported self-styled "functionalists."

Form does follow function as a matter of fact. But what of it? The term "functionalism" which so many Europeans—and their gallery in this country—use as a mere term seems to be about all that came of it for them or for anyone.

FORM FOLLOWS FUNCTION

Form follows function? Well . . . this simple fact basic to ecologist, physicist, biologist, and almost any other "ist" except the artist, has by way of discipleship to derivatives, devotees, and exploiters been razed to the level of mere dogma. The latest effects of the already trite cliché appeared as novel at the Museum of Modern Art about 1932. As this phrase was then used, we had but the latest camouflage of the old shopworn formula, "Art for art's sake." But, as said in the foreword to which this afterword is corollary, the old dogma—streamlined now—got into circulation over a hurdle of names: "cubist," "futurist," "purist," and finally "internationalist." No doubt, more names are coming. Out of the European cubo-purist or puro-cubist the modernists profess to have come into the architecture called modern—soon dubbed "internationalist." They were thrown in with me. Or vice-versa? All, originally, were minor European mirror-sects leading into or out of one bauhaus until finally, having a cart but no horse, the new slogan "form follows function" was picked up here to be used for a horse over there. Three-dimensional ideology was thus, soon by other painter-sects, degraded to sectarianism in the obvious patterns of the ever useful stencil. Instead of the new depth, another two-dimensional affair had arrived, actually no more architecture than a painter's stencil would be. But it became another aestheticism when discovered by the provincial "art elite" in our country. Call this elite the favored academic arbiters of our industrialism; of our upper haves-and-holders tending naturally, then as now, toward fascism. This elite immediately saw the stencil as the latest style and easy to use for prefabricated teaching. As promptly, the universities (advance guardians of the aesthetic and mental phases of our mass-produced imitation of a culture) imported more of it, professionalized its adoption by putting it into armchairs, and adapted its too easy (easy because superficial) advantages. Easy to learn, a cliché (or stencil) is quite as easy to forget. But nevertheless because individuality—innate sensibility—was sufficiently left out of the affair to make further academic conscription of youth quite safe (perhaps therefore), it was a great educational convenience. So, its nature not yet fully comprehended, collegiate mass-consumption of a definitely undemocratic pattern was begun in our universities and museums. It is going on there yet.

As a matter of course, to be an expedient is in the nature of what the stencil is. So in our country the stencil was soon regarded by "higher education"—itself one—as ideal. It was seen to be sufficiently "depersonalized" (to use their word for de-individualized) to be regarded as "safe"; that is to say, not sufficiently alive to be dangerous to handle or hard to teach. Nor is it yet clear to academic authority that the slogan, "form follows function," thus made available to negation by abnegation, was originally derived from a homemade affirmation of renunciation which subsequently returned to us from abroad a deformed, and so probably dangerous, import.

Now, for the sake of argument, let's again say that "form does follow function." Well . . . so does the sun rise tomorrow morning; so every bright has its dark, just as night is but a shadow cast by the sun. In all physical Nature form follows function! That is the simple fact. But too many misty cults for prestidigitators of fine-art "movements" are already fashioned of similiar simples—without due reference to their spiritual significance in Nature—for it to be ethical to let these too numerous stencilites, so recently and readily made, get away with another at expense to organic architecture.

Louis H. Sullivan would have been first to gleefully kick these self-styled functioneers —with their "A house is a machine for living" (but only if a human heart is a suction pump)—from his doorstep. In so far as his doorstep was mine I did it myself when they appeared with their dead-sea fruit, "the whited-sepulchre" (call it the flat-bosomed facade), at the Museum of Modern Art about 1932. But the affair was then far behindhand. So far behind, indeed, that where useful negation was implied it was definitely recorded by myself in so many words in the Architectural Record of February 1906 and in the many buildings which I had, by that time, designed and built. How did this fact also escape detection by "the authorities"—our own proprietary museums and learned educationists—when in 1910 it went so widely abroad as to be actually international today? Except by the circumstances peculiar to the posterior concept of culture as habitual from abroad it cannot be explained. Let us then blame the lack of vision and wisdom in the circumstances on the cross-eyed view, or jargon, and receive the return of the prodigal with a welcome proper to the wayward.

For any wanton sect to understand Louis H. Sullivan at all is to know that not then was he, nor ever would he be, for any such. His greatness for all lies in that at heart and in deed he was the great, human lyric poet whose creation out of himself of the poetic efflorescence of LOUIS H. SULLIVAN—great individual—was unique. Of course, he is best seen where happiest—seen in what he loved best: the primal plastic. Clay.

Although seeming at times a nature-ism (his danger), the idea is there: *of* the thing not *on* it; and therefore SULLIVANIAN self-expression contained the elements and prophesied organic architecture. To look down upon such efflorescence as mere "ornament" is disgraceful ignorance. We do so because we have only known ornament as self-indulgent excrescence ignorantly *applied* to some surface as a mere prettification. But, with the master, "ornament" was, like music, a matter of the soul—"of" the nature of man— inevitable to him: (natural) as leaves on trees or any fruit announced by the blossoms on the stems that carry both. It was this man that Louis H. Sullivan was and felt himself to be, that he expected me to write about someday: a far greater man than the functionalist he has been wishfully and willfully made to appear.

Actually ignorant of the proper depth of the word *Nature* as a term of the spirit, so-called internationalists dedicated the bare box to the machine god regardless and threw him in with it. These flat boxes on stilts—to further emphasize contrast to Nature (and ignorance of her quality)—were painted white to further mark aloofness not only to Nature but to man. This factish, leftish derivation of the old dictum, "Art is art precisely in that it is not Nature," by wrongly interpreting the word Nature, utterly betrayed the master's poetic sense. The third dimension which Sullivanian ornament prophesied never entered with the worshippers of "next-to-nothing" into their shrine, the whited sepulchre. When they do refer to "Nature," they deny truth by fact.

Where they build we have no place for a real man to live in unless he be purged of his own individuality. Just as in fascism we have submission of the man to exterior authority, so in this latest conventionalizing of fascist import, growing more and more mechanistic in concept and grasp, we have but a "sec." A dry next-to-nothing instead of quite something.

But negations are by nature dry. We do have a form of "restatement" of the negation of the Larkin Building, 1906, to use in the new architecture (but not to live with) in this rebottled old formula: "Art for art's sake"; in other words, a revival of the old formula, "Art is art precisely in that it is not Nature." But wholesome rejection of this certificate of divorce from Nature now posing as artistic "contrast" is our present need. Failing to match a given sample the clerk is trained to say, "Then, madam, how would you like a contrast." Concerning these old dictums, we see in them all this childish (not childlike) *misuse of the word Nature*, the use of the word as mere fact instead of a great truth, and in that misuse lies the basis for every negative sect: the expedient excuse for the architect's "Then, madam, how would you like a contrast?" The proper use of the word Nature, as *the innate character of anything or everything*, would not only void such underdone (or overdone) abstraction in the future but be useful as the spiritual cathartic necessary in times so badly underdone or overstuffed as ours.

All but a few of these negativities seem to be—or once were—painters making their advent into architecture regardless of the dignity, difficulty, and profound character of the third dimensions of actual experience in structure; therefore—no sure foundation for a new aesthetic in architecture. To bring architecture alive again as the great mother-art, negation has had its place. But its place is no longer creative. The time for affirmation is now. Nor can architecture thrive on the present. If not dated at least a decade ahead, it is born to be and stay behind its time.

Abuses notwithstanding, we must learn to use the word Nature in the proper romantic (or integral) sense of the word. Its proper use becomes indispensable if we would be free ourselves and put the true spiritual use of the word ORGANIC into the use of our language.

In this ultra-materialist era our life in Usonia needs the word used in real sense to develop honest culture of our own, or we go dry. Sap fails the graft. To take advantage of our excessive advantages our culture must be based upon decentralization and not on the major and minor axes of any grandomaniac past or modern pig-pile. Our architecture will then be in the reflex; monarchic major and minor axes no longer dominating our lives by way of any revival of any kind of "classicism," we have a chance to become a democracy. But I do not mean that organic reality—a spiritual concept—will ever degenerate to the merely realistic. The distinctions between real and realistic—between sentiment and sentimentality—between truth and fact are as important as those between the curious and the beautiful or between science and art.

HERESY

To illustrate: a great sculptor, Michael Angelo (painter), ignorant of the depth-dimensions of good construction, visualized and isolated high up in air the great masonry arch we architects call a dome. The painter—as a matter of course—provided no more to take the inevitable thrust of the mighty arched masonry-mass than the plain air over a series of tall slender upended stilts (call them columns) set up around beneath the outer rim of the great arch. The structure had to be bound with a great iron chain at a crucial moment or all would have come to the ground. Inorganic (as might be expected), this gorgeous "*tour de force*" of the painter was extraordinarily picturesque. And perhaps this rape of the arch by the picture was so extremely successful because, for most of the time before the great Angelo and totally, except for music and painting, for about five hundred years, the "Renaissance" had all but destroyed, in favor of symbolism, any integrity—that is to say, any true inner significance of architecture as sublimated structure.

How "the picture" has damaged architecture! Such pretentious artificiality as architecture had in Buonarotti's time has now got to go. Prevalent fashions in exterior symbolism already becoming less relevant came with a rush to fill the gap made as architecture became empty *"tour de force."* We now see the dome as a symbol of authority all over the world. Cultural decline has gone so far "sky-dome" by the time in which I write, the Capitol at Washington for an instance, that perhaps only some such *tour de force* could be "extraordinarily successful." The expressions of the exterior mask aided by symbolism, the long period of the rebirths of the rebirth (history calls the rebirth the Renaissance), were in this respect similar to our own period: they were going empty of Nature significance.

Organic quality in things natural to man and the earth supporting him, though likely to be miraculous, are not necessarily "mystic" and should have been less extraordinary in the thought-world of that time: a world then not yet so degenerate. But as thought (organic) was almost as rare in that day as it is in ours, the great Italian painter's rape of the arch by picture is still sensational. This ponderous anachronism styled (shall we say "streamlined") by Michael Angelo still flourishes as the symbol of authority among us so many centuries later. But now this masonry symbol is simulated—imitated—by casting iron plates in the image of the original masonry arch and bolting the iron plates securely together. The chain thus crept up to supplant the dome.

Thus—the, dome is a heresy. Throw in the pilaster, column, capital and cornice—all now Western, advertising to the world a total lack of fundamental integrity in architecture all down the line, and you will see the triumph not only of the artificial symbol of authority but the ascendancy of temporal authority over the principles of democracy. With this new integrity which we call the "third dimension" (call the third "depth") in mind—and—yes—you *are* on the way to a fourth dimension; headed for dimensions at will. Structural integrity seems even more than ever absent from the so-called modern architecture of our national scene. Is this because the third dimension inevitable to organic structure has so defied the camera eye (or the glass eye of the classicist) that it has also defied, or is derided by the flat vision of our stencilists? Their sentimental worship of the Greeks would so indicate. Nevertheless the sense of *depth* which we are here calling the third dimension—a spiritual quality that cannot be forced but must be wooed—marries the building to human life and weds both to the ground. Architecture in this deeper sense is not formidable but is truly fundamental to democracy. We will find the democratic home to be integral part of the man himself, placed upon his own share of earth, and building there a hearth he can call his own and look himself in the face. To that prophetic expression of himself man must cling for salvation in the heedless voracity of this epidemic, machine-mad, money-power era. No posterior cliché for building that sidesteps to evade or contradict the Nature of man as a noble integral feature of his native and natural environment can flourish today if we are to survive as a democratic people. No stencil-*ist* or any ist—even the artist—has power to realize this primal element of organic character in a building: character seen as individuality. Negation, when habitual, is so soon lifeless—too soon a standardization leading to utter mediocrity. Stagnation. Stagnate architecture—the mother-art—and stagnation will go on into all branches of all the great arts and the great arts are the heart of our civilized life. Then life lies—where? We cannot live on science.

Timely building no less than timely man must be courageously affirmative! Affirmation is infinitely more difficult than negation. Affirm the truth that great building must become great art—innate living-feature of man's environment as bees, trees, or flowers are of his earth; say that a great building must be a great natural: a reality for man—not realistic or a contrast but affirmative as man himself is in true democracy. If the modern man in Usonia is to enjoy culture true to his own time and to this democratic ideal of freedom, our buildings must be groundlings. They may dramatize what and as they please, but only the good ground can give validity to the drama; give it by loving the building. Any cliché hates the ground. So the ground hates the cliché.

IDEAS

Ideas are also manifestations of Nature.

If democracy prevails among nations then, within this ideal of the ideal we call an organic architecture, the culture of each and every country must "grow its own." Democracy, likewise, must be *grown*. Its culture especially cannot live very long on the prohibition or negation. Neither democracy nor organic architecture can ever be enforced.

Instead of the trite fact of the dogma, "form follows function," in order to be truly significant of the master's thought let us learn the dramatic truth that *"form and function are one,"* recognizing what the phrase means when we use it. It means that a *building can only be functional when integral with environment and so formed in the nature of materials according to purpose and method* as to be a living entity true each in all to all: no small order. But, thus believing, we will gradually learn to express and expand the thought of the great lyric poet—that was Louis H. Sullivan. His end is not yet. By deference and implication we will then go far to prevent a slogan, already a decadent dogma, from disastrous encroachment upon our native gifts.

The laws of God are to be read in the laws
of Nature.
Only love of truth can restore to us the
liberties we have lost.

Since fascist-tainted propaganda for a style suited to authority began in our museums and universities some twenty years ago, I have foreseen ultimate issue between architecture thus made useful to academic authority, easy to teach, and architecture natural to our needs as a democratic people—to be inspired but not taught—and so of slow growth. To lighten the mystery of this unintelligible world we need architecture communicative of an ideal flowing from individual to individual, not as formalism but in the reflex as innate individuality. Only so inspired to become fit abode for the soul of man, will our buildings ever rise above the shed, a bogus palace, the flat-bosomed facade, or some monument authority builds to honor authority—and this nation learn to build as a free democracy.

All "*ites*" and "*isms*," especially individual*isms*, invalidate individuality. Without exception they are making and can only make facades suited to dictatorial power. We have seen in the provincial imitations of imported point, line, and plane nothing organic, but a modernism: degeneracy grasping for salvation by the kind of machine worship that brings man himself to the level of machines. Nature herself covets and cherishes variety and dreads reiteration unqualified. She goes to great lengths to achieve infinite variety. There is something sinister for the living in the beating of the drum. Unrelieved, it is the song of death.

FACT

Although the building may be a piece of property, by now our modern society should be so far developed as to realize that an architect's work is the noblest of all utilities and should be of the very texture, substance, and spirit of our own culture. Though his art is most basic and profound of all the great arts, at the same time architecture is the great art least understood in modern times. Not until democracy really learns to build unconcerned with a style—a style is reiteration—but build inspired by the Nature of style itself will our culture develop architecture or even men able to comprehend it. The camera-eye of science is too flat. The fact is not the truth.

Therefore, because this affair of the third dimension is less objective than subjective—thickness seen as depth being a matter as difficult in words as a fourth dimension would be in our present mathematics—this belated book may not be easy to read. When our culture is our own it will contain the vocabulary necessary to that architecture freshly conceived—disciplined from *within* by principle.*

* The Japanese, their culture nearest of all peoples to Nature, use words like:

Edaburi—the habit-pattern of procedure from stem to leaf to bud to blossom and to fruit—what it is that makes, say, the pine tree a pine as distinguished from a cherry tree or an oak. They say it with a word.

Shibui—a subjective quality at first repellent in a work of art, but for some reason you are impelled to go back for a second look, begin to see something you missed ... go back to be fascinated by extraordinary beauty. They say it in a word.

Notan—the nearest translation is the Italian word *chiaroscuro*—but *notan* is not only shading, but the swelling or fading of the tint on something that is itself. Saying so we do not convey the subtle integral effect that is *notan*.

This book is a graph, it is true—neither biograph nor autobiograph but a combination of both. Here on its pages is the work-life of a great master and the pencil in his hand—myself. You will find no concern with architecture in two dimensions fashioned like some brass hat for the head to supplant a natural head of hair, but architecture in the depth-dimension that is completely integral: of and natural to the nature of the circumstance. Organic architecture is therefore the growth in space of an idea—a state of mind proceeding by the natural science of structure in the use of materials to the splendid, appropriate art of FORM: form true to purpose. Furthermore it is the art of building wherein aesthetic and construction *not only approve but prove each other*. In organic sense such building is an entity of the human spirit as that of any tree or flower is of the ground. A natural, human circumstance—possible only to the complete architect. There will never be too many of him. He is master of the elements: earth, air, fire, light, and water. Space, motion, and gravitation are his palette: the sun his brush. His concern is the heart of humanity. He, of all men, must see into the life of things; know their honor.

Frank Lloyd Wright   Taliesin

TWENTY ADDITIONAL DRAWINGS

THIS SECTION CONTAINS HITHERTO UNPUBLISHED DRAWINGS,
NINETEEN BY LOUIS SULLIVAN AND ONE BY FRANK LLOYD WRIGHT

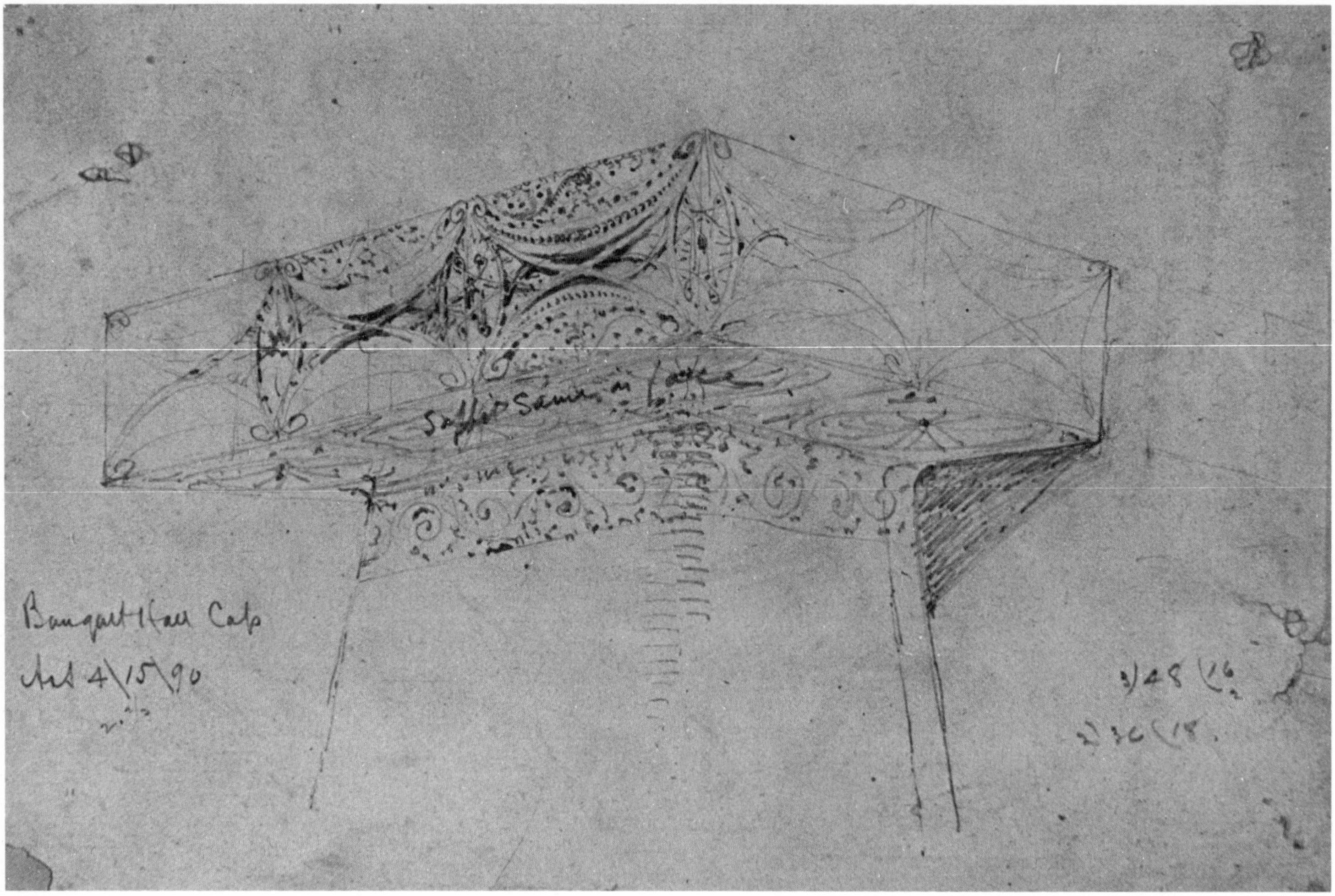

 Banquet hall capital. ("soffit same as face"). 1890

(Facing page) Bronze gates. Getty Tomb. Ink drawing by Frank Lloyd Wright, with notes signed by FLLW. Undated

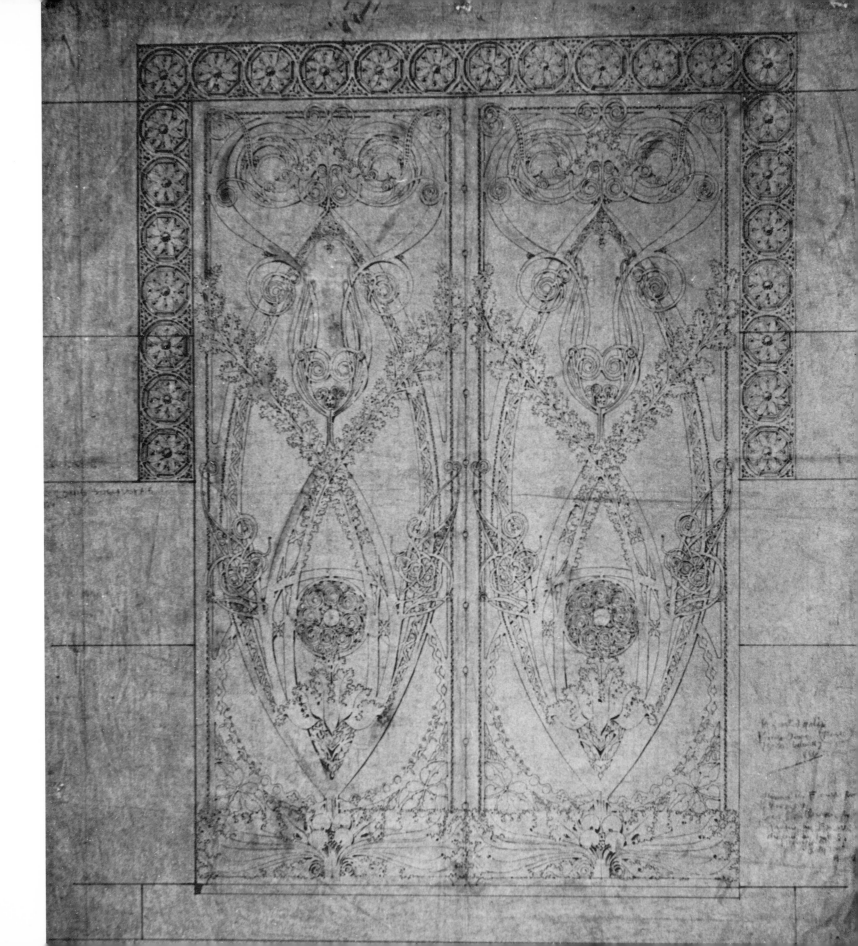

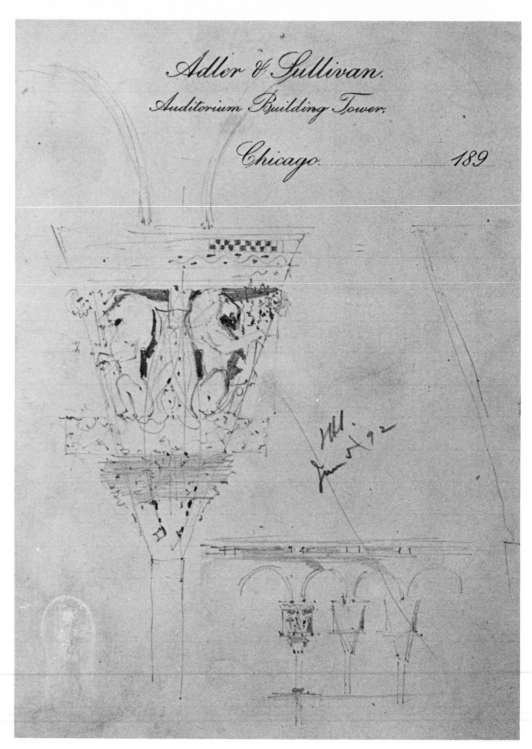

Adler & Sullivan.
Auditorium Building Tower.
Chicago 189

Study for column capital. 1892

Study for ornamental frieze. Bronze gates. Getty Tomb. Undated

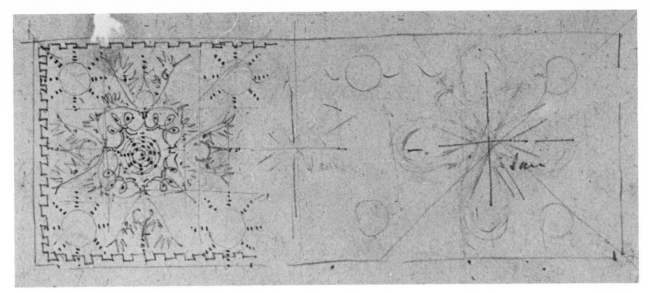

Studies. 1893

Railing block. Chicago Stock Exchange Building. 1894

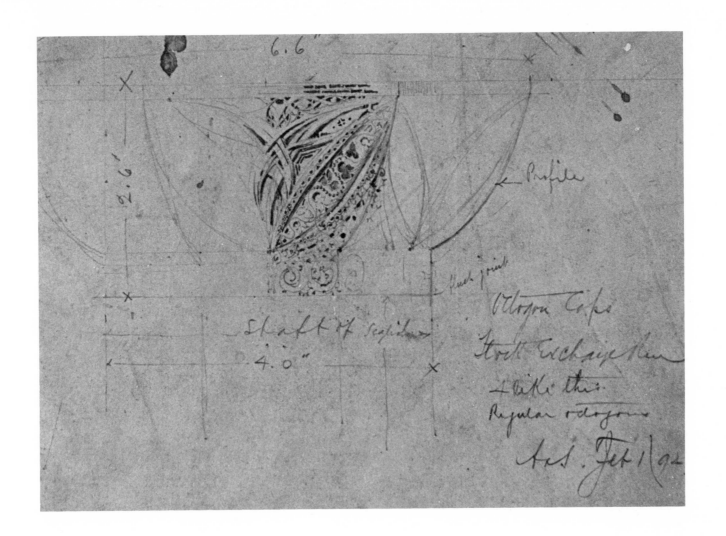

One of four octagon capitals. Chicago Stock Exchange Building. 1894 **175**

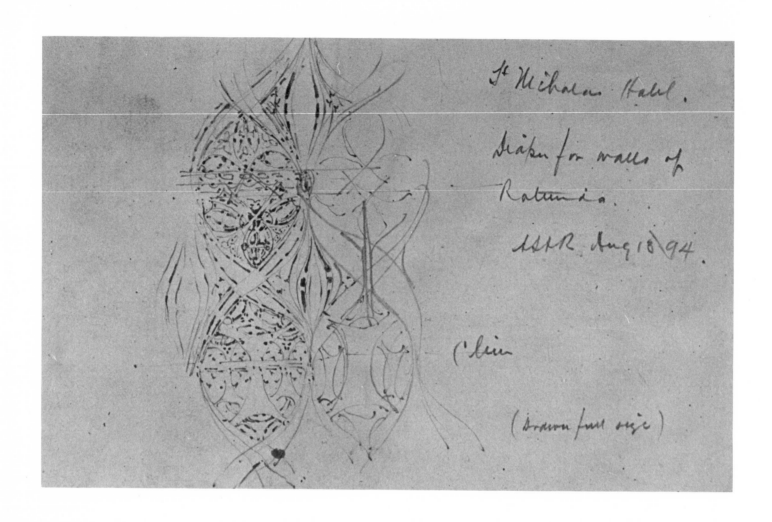

Diaper for walls of rotunda. St. Nicholas Hotel. 1894   (Facing page, left) ("12" Borders"). St. Nicholas Hotel. 1894

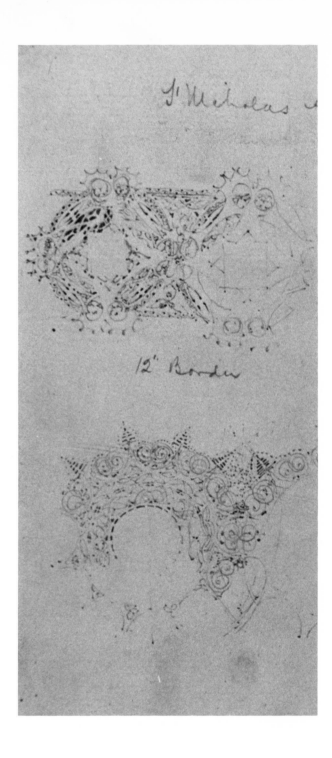

Sketch for iron fence. 1899   **177**

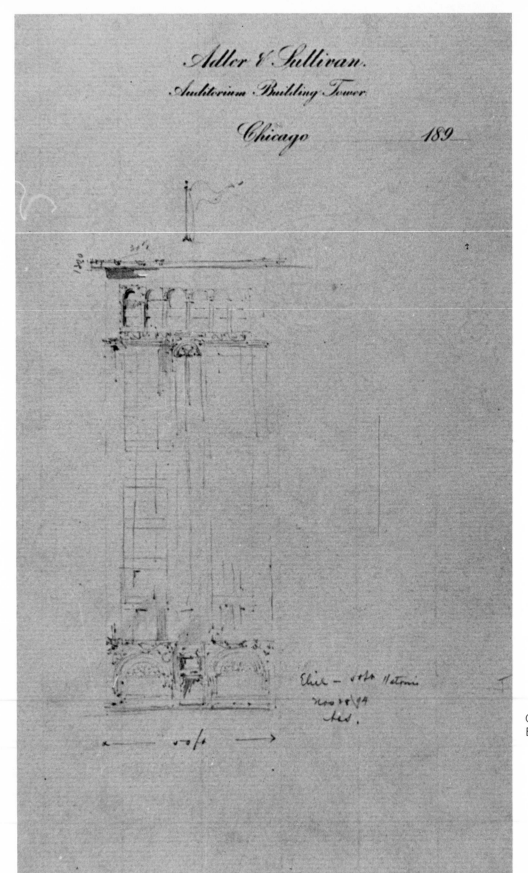

Conceptual sketch, skyscraper.
Eliel Building, Chicago. 1894

Study, carved wainscot.
(Note by FLLW). Undated

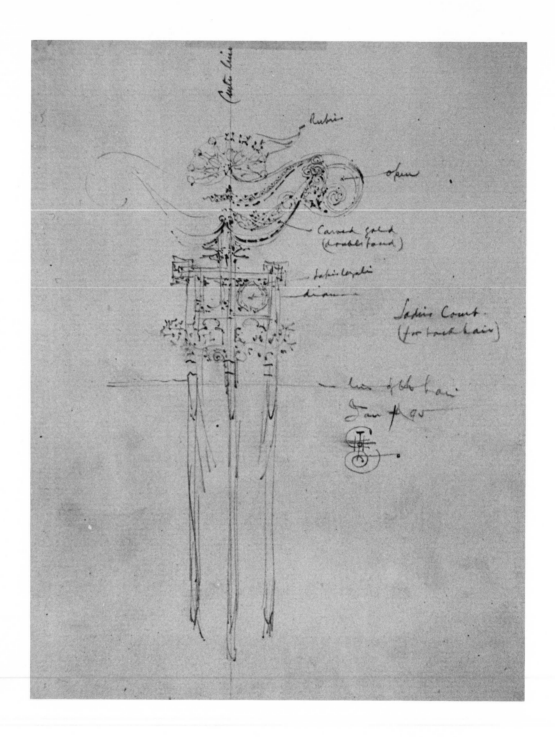

180   ''Ladies comb for back hair.'' Carved gold (double faced), rubies, lapis lazuli, diamonds. 1895

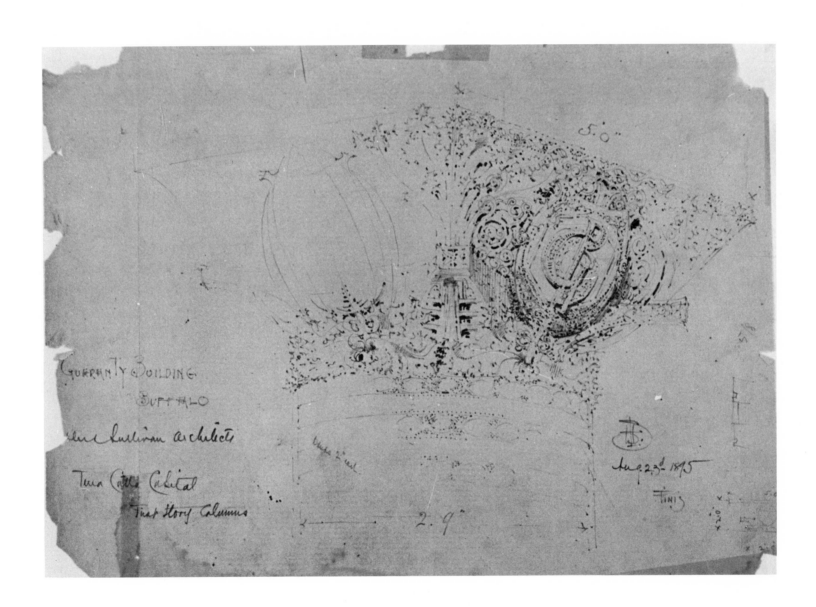

Capital for first story columns. Terra cotta. Guaranty Building. 1895 **181**

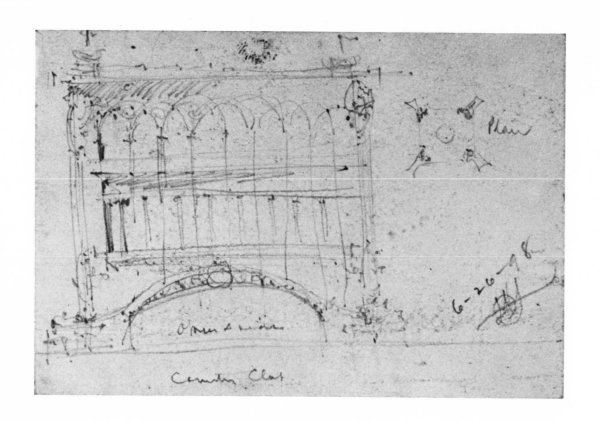

Sketch for elevation and plan of country club.
Drawn on back of business card, 4½'' x 3''. 1898

(Facing page, top) Monogram design. University
of Michigan. 1895. (Bottom) Study for clock, National Farmers' Bank, Owatonna, Minnesota 1907

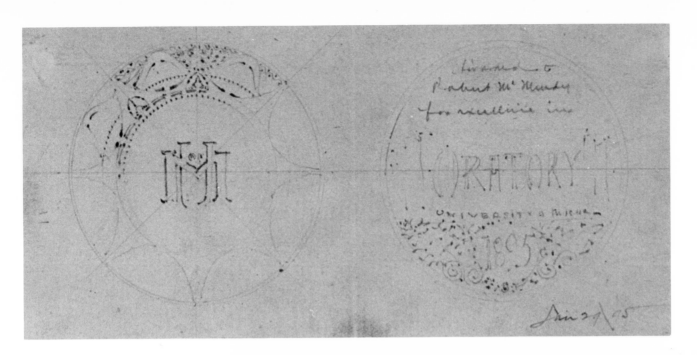

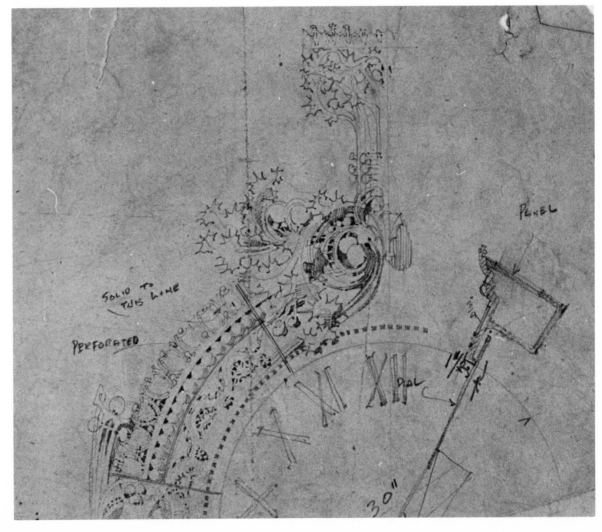

VOLUME TWO: NUMBER FOUR

GIBSON'S MAGAZINE

MARCH
·1910·

PRICE TEN CENTS

FEB 11-10

Design for cover of Gibson's
Magazine, March issue. 1910

THE PHOTOGRAPHS

THIS SECTION IS DESIGNED TO SHOW DETAILS OF LOUIS SULLIVAN'S ORNAMENT IN EXECUTED STRUCTURES, WITH VIEWS OF THE BUILDINGS INCLUDED AS CONTEXT. THE PHOTOGRAPHS, SELECTED FROM THE WORK OF JAMES BLAIR, ASAO DOI, LEN GITTLEMAN, PAUL HASSEL, LEON LEWANDOWSKI, RICHARD NICKEL, ALVIN LOGINSKY AND AARON SISKIND, WERE MADE IN THE PROJECT SUPERVISED BY AARON SISKIND AT THE INSTITUTE OF DESIGN, ILLINOIS INSTITUTE OF TECHNOLOGY.

186   Auditorium Building, Chicago. 1887-89

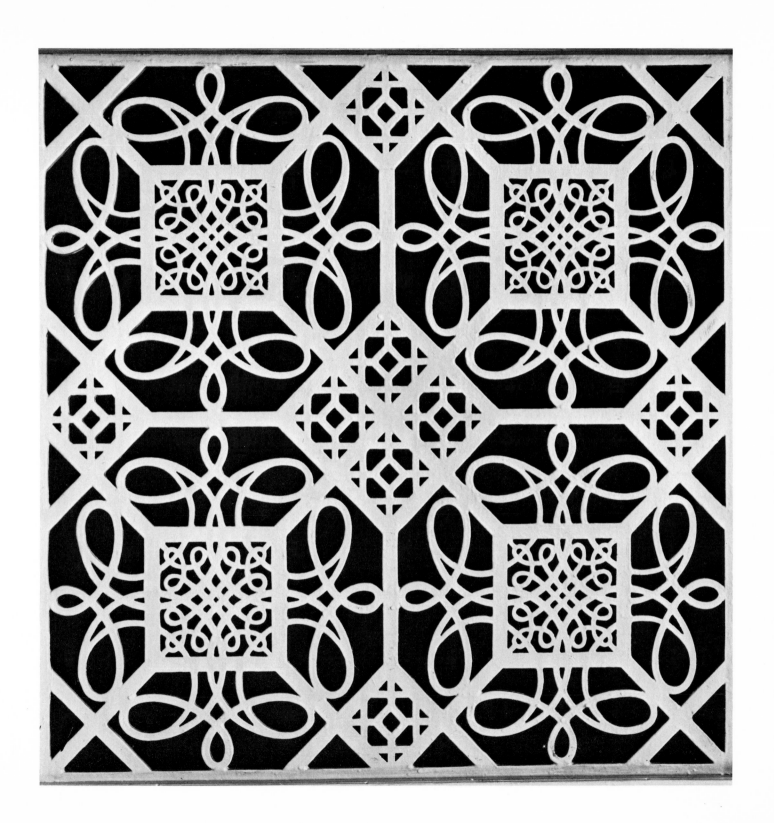

Fret-sawed wooden screen, upper part of door between main dining room and kitchen. Auditorium hotel   **187**

Auditorium

Theatre mural frame. Auditorium

(Above) Detail, Auditorium dining room. (Left) Stencil on upper wall, staircase landing, Auditorium theatre. (Facing page) Detail (colored tessera), first landing of grand staircase. Auditorium hotel

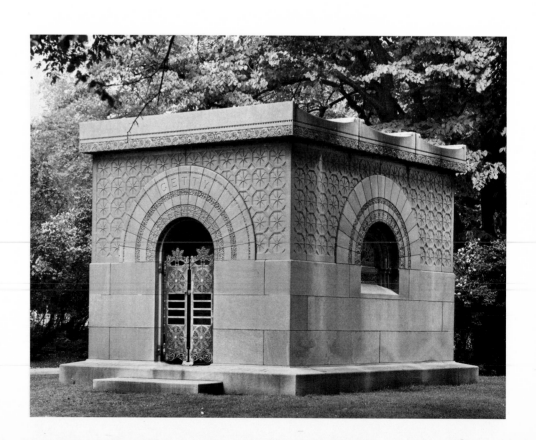

196   Getty Tomb, Graceland Cemetery, Chicago. 1890

Details, exterior and door. Getty Tomb

197

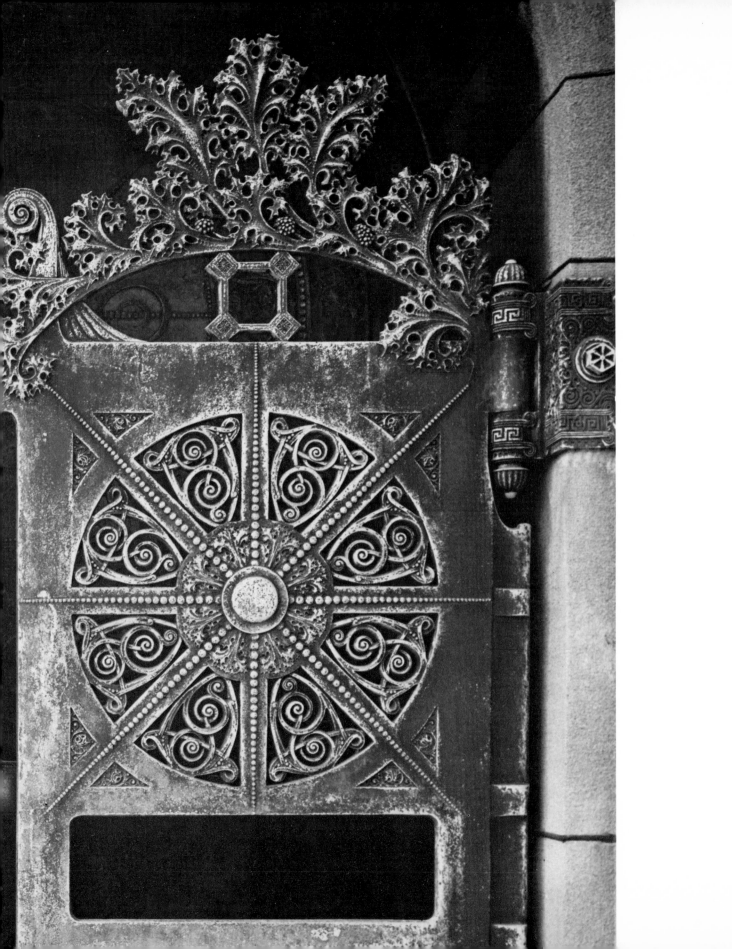

Wainwright Building, St. Louis. 1890-91. (Facing page) Detail

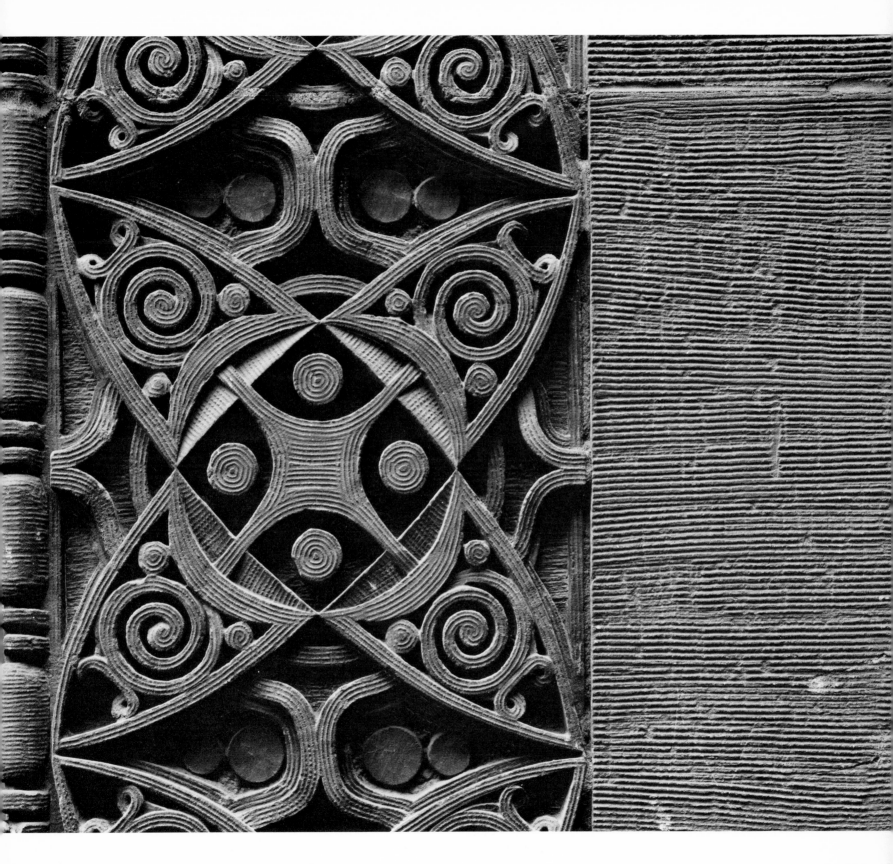

201

204   Schiller (later called Garrick Theatre) Building, Chicago. 1891-92

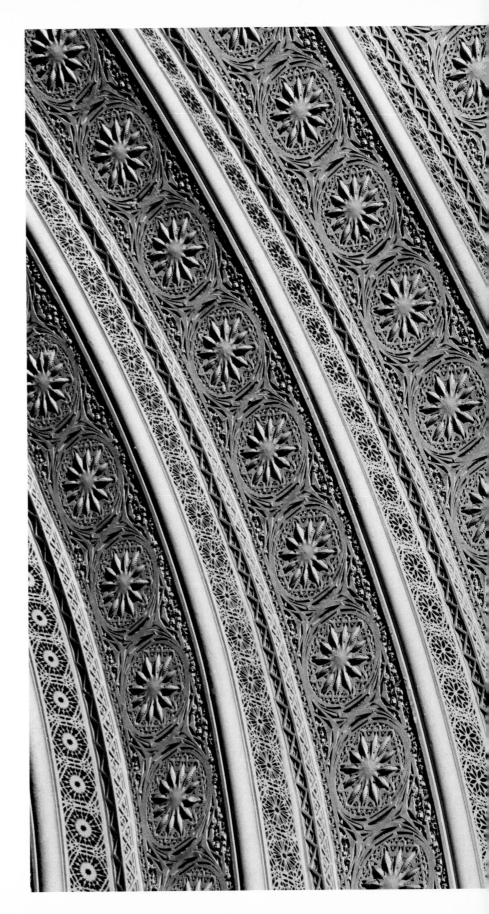

Theatre and interior detail

206 Wainwright Tomb, Bellefontaine Cemetery, St. Louis. 1892. (Facing page) Exterior detail

Stock Exchange Building, Chicago. 1893-94. (Below) Exterior detail. (Facing page) Detail, elevator grill

Guaranty (later called Prudential) Building, Buffalo.
1894-95. (Right) Exterior detail. (Facing page) Doorplate

214   Condict (later called Bayard) Building, New York City. 1897-98.

Gage Building, Chicago. 1898-99. (Facing page) Fascia detail

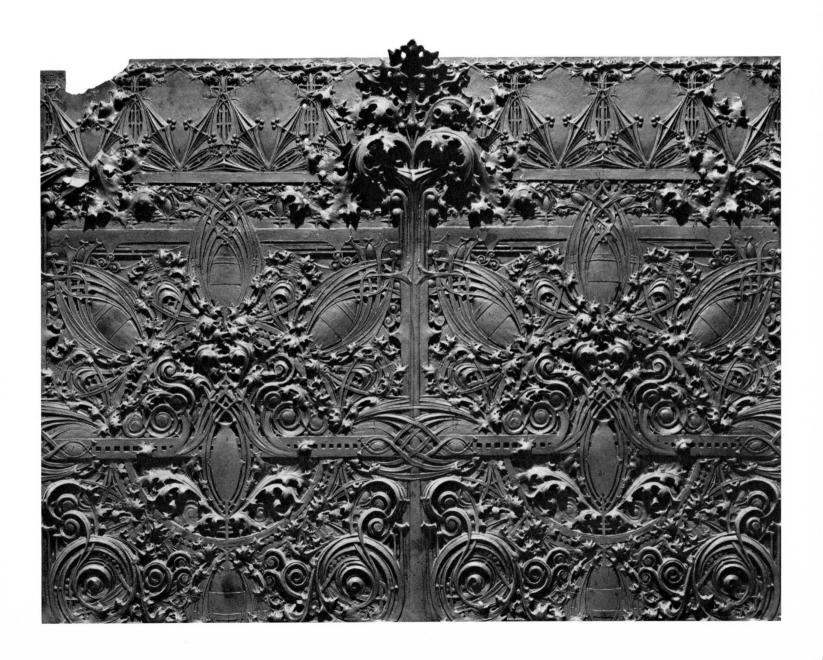

217

Schlesinger & Mayer Department Store (later called Carson Pirie Scott), Chicago. 1899-1906. (Facing page) Entrance detail

Schlesinger & Mayer Store exterior views: (facing page) cast-
iron column facing and (below) detail above display window

222   National Farmers' (later called Security) Bank, Owatonna, Minnesota. 1907-08. (Facing page) Interior view

Detail, above entrance

228   People's Savings & Loan Association Bank, Sidney, Ohio. 1917-18

Exterior detail

Farmers' & Merchants' Union Bank, Columbus, Wisconsin. 1919. (Facing page) Exterior detail

William P. Krause Music Store, Chicago. 1922

BY LOUIS H. SULLIVAN

TWO ESSAYS ON THE IMPERIAL HOTEL

CONCERNING THE IMPERIAL HOTEL, TOKYO, JAPAN

On the vast stage of the world drama, two ideas both of them immense in power, confront each other in spectacular appeal to the fears and the courage of mankind. And it is precisely this condition that gives animus and validity to what is to follow in contemplation of the Imperial Hotel, of Tokyo, Japan, as a high act of courage—an utterance of man's free spirit, a personal message to every soul that falters, and to every heart that hopes.

It is becoming clear that a new thought is arising in the world which is destined to displace the old thought. The new thought partakes of the nature of that freedom of which men long have dreamed. It is now breaking through the crust of the old thought which thus far in history has dominated the world of men and which embodies the idea of dominion and of submissive acquiescence.

The old idea, or fetish, is dying because it no longer satisfies the expansion of thought and feeling of which the impressive revelation of modern science are a primary factor; and especially because it is no longer at one with those instincts we call human; it does not recognize the heart as a motive power.

Yet is the old idea tenaciously fixed in the minds of a majority of those engaged in commerce, the industries, the law, the courts of justice, and especially among parasites of all kinds and degrees.

The old idea reaches from top to bottom of the social strata, and also from bottom to top. It is an age-old fixed idea, based upon a concept of self preservation, which once may have had an outward semblance of validity even though its stability of superstructure rested upon a foundation of human slavery, ignorance and suppression.

While in modern times bodily slavery as such has been done away with in theory, the old idea has persisted, curiously transformed into a slavery of the mind, which also ranges through all the social strata, even as men appear to be bodily free.

This new slavery of mind is manifest in a strange, ever-present disturbing fear, anxiety, and incertitude, which permeates society and which leads the individual to cling for safety to the old ideas, superstitions, and taboos, in order that he may conform and not appear too obvious as an individual, a target; that he may, above all, escape the fashionable epithets, "crank", "visionary", "dreamer", "freak". Hence comes about a new economic slavery causing the man, high or low, to fear for his job, and live in a nightmare so terrifying that he dare not say one word that might be construed as disturbing. Such minds in their nature are asleep to the significance of great world movements in thought.

But the idea of freedom is also old; older indeed than the slave-idea. For it is of the nature of any organism that it wishes to be free to grow and expand. This instinctive desire for freedom has been held in check and dominated by the intellectual idea of fear, resulting in unnumbered inhibitions and suppressions, which have led to an obscuration of the minds of men of the two ideas of slavery and freedom.

But the idea of freedom also is beginning to permeate the thoughts of men, with a new urge, also through all the strata of society, and is massively defining, taking form, and becoming energized, through an ever-growing knowledge and ever-increasing understanding of the true nature, the true status of man not as creature but creator; an enlarging view of man's inherent powers and a growing consciousness that his slavery has been self-imposed. It was in this sense that I have had occasion recently to comment upon the splendid interpretation of the spirit of the American people manifest in the design submitted in the competition for the Tribune Building in Chicago—by a Finlander—Eliel Saarinen.

It is in this sense that we are now about to contemplate the new Imperial Hotel in Tokyo, Japan.

This great work is the masterpiece of Frank Lloyd Wright, a great free spirit, whose fame as a master of ideas is an accomplished world-wide fact.

Through prior visits he had discerned, and added to the wealth of his own rich nature, the spirit, as evidenced in forms of the ideals of Old Japan, which still persist, in slumber, among its living people, needing but the awakening touch.

It is a high faculty of what we call genius to penetrate and temporarily to reside within the genius of another people foreign to our own local ways. And it is this quality of vision, this receptivity, this openness of mind, that especially signalizes the free spirit—the mind free from provincialism and the fear of life.

Next in order to the power of vision comes the power to interpret in thought; and, next to this, the power to express the thought, the state of feeling, in concrete terms.

In this structure is not to be found a single form distinctly Japanese; nor that of any other country; yet in its own individual form, its mass, and subsidiaries, its evolution of plan and development of thesis; in its sedulous care for niceties of administration, and for the human sense of joy, it has expressed, in inspiring form as an epic poem, addressed to the Japanese people, their inmost thought. It is characterized by the quality, Shibui, a Japanese word, signifying the reward of earnest contemplation. In studying the concrete expression, the embodiment of idea in solid form, the magnitude of this structure should always be borne in mind. It is 300 x 500 feet on the ground, the area thus equaling 150,000 square feet, or nearly two and one-half times the area covered by the great Auditorium Building in Chicago. The structure is three stories high in the main, with special masses equivalent in height to seven stories.

In a sense it is a huge association of structures, a gathering of the clans, so to speak; it is a seeming aggregate of buildings shielding beauteous gardens, sequestered among them. Yet there hovers over all, and as an atmosphere everywhere, a sense of primal power in singleness of purpose; a convincing quiet that bespeaks a master hand, guiding and governing.

Upon further analysis, aided by reference to the floor plans, it is disclosed that the structure is not a group, but a single mass; spontaneously subdividing into subsidiary forms in groups or single, as the main function itself flows into varied phases, each seeking expression in appropriate correlated forms, each and all bearing evidence of one controlling mind, of one hand moulding materials like a master craftsman.

It is this coming to grips with realities that infiltrates the mind of the observer, until he feels the reward of earnest contemplation in the sense that what at first he had regarded as a material structure is sending forth to him an emanation of beauty, the presence of a living thing, a wondrous contribution to the architecture of the world, an exposition of the virile thought of modern man. So much for the ever-growing fascination of external forms, which appear as eloquent expressions of a something that must reside within them and justify them, upon logical grounds, as forms developed from functions of utility.

In considerations both of analysis and synthesis one must regard the plan as the mainspring of the work; and this plan in turn as but the organiza-tion of the primal purposes of utility, manifold in their nature, of service to be rendered.

Now, in examining the plans at the various floor levels, one discovers that the big idea of service divides into two specialized forms: the first constituting as a complex group a hotel complete in all details for the comfort and entertainment of the traveling public, or residentials; the second, more formal and sumptuous part, is discernible as a group embodiment of the necessity for a clearing-house not only for the social obligations incurred by Japanese official life in its contacts with representatives of other lands, but also for the great social functions now inevitable in the high life of the Capital.

Consequent upon the relation of these two groups there exists a most felicitous system of interpenetrations, and communications, with a circulatory system, all worked out in a manner signifying not only mental grasp but creative imagination, based on the human being as a unit and a motive.

The dispositions throughout the entire building are so dexterously interwoven that the structure as a whole becomes a humanized fabric, in any part of which one feels the all-pervading sense of continuity, and of intimate relationships near and far. In this especial sense the structure, carrying the thought, is unique among hotel buildings throughout the world. Japan is to be felicitated that its superior judgment in the selection of an architect of masterly qualifications, of such nature as to welcome new problems of time and place, has been justified. The longer the contemplation of this work is continued, the more intense becomes the conviction that this Master of Ideas has not only performed a service of distinction, but, far and above this, has presented to the people of Japan, as a free-will offering, a great gift which shall endure for all generations to come as a world exemplar, most beautiful and inspiring, of which Japan may well be proud among the nations as treasuring it in sole possession.

In further study of the plans in their aspect of economics, one should carefully note the differences of levels, shown thereon but more clearly set forth in the longitudinal section. These differences of level are, in one aspect, a part of the charm of the work considered from the human point of view, and, technically, as a skillful method of deployment. They favor also the interpenetrations and the easy accessibility of the larger units and, thus, the compactness of arrangement and economy of space. A notable feature in this regard is the location of a single great kitchen, centrally placed in such wise as to serve the cabaret directly, the main restaurant directly, the private dining rooms by stairways and capacious electric service elevators, and likewise the banquet hall and ballroom above.

Beneath the banquet hall is a theatre seating 1,000, and at the level of the main floor of the theatre the entire structure is traversed and in a manner bisected by a grand promenade twenty feet in width and 300 feet in length. This promenade brings the two long wings of guest rooms in touch with the central group and acts as a foyer from which are entered the theatre, four groups of private dining rooms, and opposite the theatre a large parlor, the projecting balcony of which overlooks the restaurant. The floor of the promenade is sixteen feet above sidewalk level. Beneath the promenade at the north end is situated the formal social entrance with attendant service rooms and hallway leading to passenger elevators. Spaciously around the intersection point of the axis of the promenade with the central axis of the grand-plan are grouped stairways, passenger elevators, service elevators, service stairs, and other utilities. Within this group the service element is logically vertical. Elsewhere the circulation is mainly in the horizontal sense, as there are but three tiers of guest rooms.

The two great wings, each 500 feet in length, contain the guest rooms, 285 in number, to be hereinafter described. These two huge parallel masses act as guardians of the inner courts, the gardens, and the more open structural effects, protecting them against the heavy prevailing winds and insuring a large measure of quiet, a sense of retirement and relief from a busy and noisy world without.

There remains to be considered an introductory group, placed within the open space bounded by the main guest wings and the formal social group, and lying symmetrically along the main axis of the grand-plan. It is connected to the wings by means of open bridges over terraces, leading to elevators and stairways. This group constitutes the welcoming feature of a grandiose and most hospitable plan—a plan based upon a rare sense of human nature, everywhere discernible throughout the structure.

At the western, or initial, beginning of the grand-plan, the parallel wings throw out minor wings of an enfolding character. Between these two wings lies a large formal pool, on each side of which are the driveways for automobiles. For jinrikishas separate entrances and runs are provided through the main wings. The entrance feature of the central group stands well back from the pool.

One ascends a few steps and enters a spacious vestibule, from which lead up and down special stairways. A broad flight carries one to the main lobby from which one may enter the lounges, the side wings, or directly ahead, the main restaurant. At higher levels the group contains tea rooms, library, roof garden; and below, the executive offices, the bazaar, and the swimming pool. Beautiful form combinations and vistas make the interior treatment highly interesting and inviting. The level of the restaurant floor is seven feet above the sidewalk grade and nine feet below the grand promenade. The latter is reached from it by means of stairways, upper-level terraces or by elevators.

It cannot too often be reiterated that the terrace idea is the key to the development of the plan in its entirety and that this idea, seized upon by the constructive creative imagination, and carried into logical and beautiful extension, reveals the secret of the serenity and joy of this edifice. Nowhere is the sense of size oppressive, for the eye finds interest everywhere. Thus the structure may truly be called epic, as one views its large simplicity of utterance and richness of well ordered detail. Peculiarly entrancing in this latter regard is the treatment of the lava within and without the structure. Everywhere its surface is wrought in intricate pattern. Constantly varying in expression in accord with location, and so beautifully conceived and cut as to appear of it, integral with it, not applied. The effect is of a continuous, velvety shimmer of lava surface.

Among functional details are to be noted the system of external night-lighting, organically incorporated in large perforated units within the masonry at carefully considered strategic points; the terraced bridges which seem to float; the sump-tuous treatment of the entrance to the social group; the recognition of the terminals of elevator shafts and dumbwaiters. These latter utilitarian things are not hidden or denied, they are affirmed, as they should be, and add to the fullness and fidelity of expression. Indeed, it seems to be but little understood that fidelity to the finer truths inhering in material things is of the essence of romance. And this is a romantic edifice, heroic, dramatic and lyric in expression of function and of form.

A notable selection of local materials has been adopted for the external effects: hand-made brick and hewn lava are chiefly used with a most interesting interspersion of copper for the cornices and delicately worked copper roofs. All flat roofs are of concrete and are treated as gardens.

The color effect is quiet, yet piquant. The bricks are buff, the lava greenish yellow with deep brown spots, the copper turquoise. Minor color effects are secured in various materials, while to all of these effects appertains the added charm of gardens, and distributed shrubs and flowers—all of which are daily cared for; and potted and vased effects are renewed as occasion requires and the changing seasons suggest.

The general construction of the building is definitely based upon the reinforced-concrete-slab idea, carried out by the architect theoretically and practically to its limits, in a manner so novel, so logical, so convincing, as to be of the highest technical interest to those familiar with the general slab idea. The specific application here has to do directly with a flexible resistance to earth-quakes—developing shocks, undulations, oscillations, and twists, in action.

The entire structure rests upon a layer of spongy soil, beneath which is found mud of undetermined depth. Short concrete piles are inserted in the upper layer, where required and as numerous as required, capped by reinforced concrete slabs which receive their direct loads at calculated points. The entire structure thus rests upon a flexible foundation which is free to yield to the mutations of earthquake disturbance and come back to place again.

By a system of distribution of steel rods everywhere the masonry superstructure is knitted thoroughly together in such wise as to render it yielding but resilient, hence secure against fracture or distortion. The slabs are as tenaciously yet flexibly adjusted to the vertical supports, and, where occasion requires, the slab system merges from the concept of lintel into that of cantilever. There is here so general a use of this latter method, on account of its adaptability to projecting horizontal slabs otherwise unsupported and the resulting ease of creating unobstructed areas, that it may perhaps be described as in essence a reinforced-cantilever-slab-system.

In the construction of all outer walls wooden forms were dispensed with; the outer layer of specially notched bricks, and the inside layer of hollow bricks, serving as such. In the cavity between, rods, vertical and horizontal, were placed, and then the concrete filler, the wall thus becoming a solid mass of varied materials, into which the floor slabs are so solidly tied as to take on the character of cantilevers, as conditions of disturbance might demand.

Thus we have a structure almost literally hand made—the use of machinery having proved relatively inefficient—a structure so solidly built of materials inseparably united as to possess all the virtues of a monolith, and yet so completely threaded through with steel fibres as to add the virtues of elasticity and resilience.

The policy of administration of actual construction work was based upon the traditional habits of the Japanese skilled laborer and craftsman. These active and tireless little men are so deft and nimble that results were most thorough, even though at first they required instruction in the use of materials with which they were not familiar.

This structure, designed theoretically and worked out practically to withstand distortion or fracture by earthquake, was put to the test while nearing completion in April, 1922, in broad daylight, during the heaviest temblor in point of severity Japan had known in fifty years. Wide destruction was wrought in the city of Tokyo. The shock was terrific. The Imperial was violently jolted. It visibly trembled, swayed and rocked in the upheaval, and at its ending quietly steadied to position, free of distortion, rents or damage of any kind.

So much for a system of construction altogether novel in conception and execution, carried out by a strong, persistent mind, as imaginative in its insight into fundamental principles of engineering as in its profound insight into the romance of breathing life and beauty, humanity and spirit, into forms and materials otherwise helplessly inert.

It is thus that the master mind works, to bring forth, out of the fabric of a dream, a fabric of enduring reality. As to the interior, a noteworthy feature is the use of lava and brick in the grand promenade, the theatre, the restaurant and the banquet hall. It was a happy thought to penetrate the interior with materials of the exterior, thus giving a sense of enduring construction.

The equipment is thorough and complete; electric heating, light and motive power, the usual telephone service, and a system of mechanical ventilation constantly in use and so arranged as to deliver cooler air in summer. All furniture, rugs and hangings of the public rooms are of special design, simple, strong and rich, partaking of the character and specifically related to the forms of the structure in a fine play of polychrome.

The guest room arrangement of the wings has been worked out to conserve space, concentrate conveniences and preserve a quiet effect. The rooms are not large, but are arranged and furnished to become sitting rooms; the beds are in evidence more as couches than as beds. The typical small room is 15 by 18, with a 6 by 10 bathroom deducted. The typical large room is 15 by 22, bathroom similarly deducted. Average ceiling height 9 feet 4 inches. The electric heating and indirect lighting are combined in a standard attached to twin tables in the center of each room. These tables have a small writing table and a small tea table beneath them which may be removed to any part of the room, and, when not in use, may be returned to their places as part of the central group. The electric heat is thus at the center of the room.

The wardrobe is a built-in feature of each bedroom, and is designed to accommodate a steamer trunk, a wardrobe trunk and two suit cases.

It has ample hanging space for clothes and the drawers of the old-fashioned dresser have been worked into this feature. There is storage space above it for purchases. A feature of this wardrobe is a guest-box accessible from the corridor or the bedroom at the will of the guest. This guest-box also contains the telephone. A full length mirror is placed against the side wall, and a small dressing table placed beside it. The central group of tables and this dressing table, together with an overstuffed easy chair or two, a light, wooden chair or two, and a hassock, are all the furniture of the room, except the couch-beds. It will be seen in this arrangement that great simplicity has been arrived at. An individual color scheme characterizes each room. A specially designed rug to correspond is upon the floor.

The furniture covering, bed covers and window hangings are of the same stuff and color, and correspond in each case with the color note of the room. The color scheme ranges through the whole gamut of color from quiet grays to bright rose and old blue or gold.

The effect of the whole is quiet and complete. Everywhere there is ample light. Privacy is insured by the omission of the transom and the device of the guest-box. Cross-ventilation is secured in every room and bathroom by means of forced draught acting through ducts and a series of square ventilators set in the corridor partition above the picture rail. These are easily adjusted for summer or winter use.

The corridor ceilings are all dropped beneath the concrete slabs to make continuous ducts, to which are connected the vertical vent shafts between every pair of rooms. These vertical shafts extend from basement to attic space and contain pipes and wiring, which are accessible and free of the construction everywhere. The bathroom is an adjunct of the bedroom; in every case treated as a part of it. It is lined with ivory colored mosaic tiles, all external and internal corners curved. The bathtub is a sunken pool in the floor of the room, formed, with curved corners, of the same mosaic tile as the floor and the walls. The room has a vaulted ceiling, and screened windows in the outer wall. The whole is drained and impervious to water in every part. The floor is electrically heated from below.

The main corridors of the guest wings are six feet wide, exposing the brick-faced concrete piers that support the floor, giving to the whole the effect of a cloistered promenade. The corridors are artificially lighted through perforated metal screens set into the ceiling.

The corridor floors are cork-tiled. The threshold has everywhere been eliminated. Where plaster has been used the walls are treated with ground pearl shell splashed on to a heavy coat of paint in the Japanese manner. All the windows in the building are screened, shaded and curtained. The woods, where used in the trimming, is throughout of Hokkaido oak, waxed. Outside each large room is a tiled balcony or terrace reached by low windows opening upon it. Baggage rooms, in each wing, for the storage of guests' luggage, easily accessible at any time, are located next to the elevators on the general level.

Thus an attempt has been made by this writer to set forth as clearly as may be the nature of a great work of architectural art founded in this particular case upon the utilities associated with human needs, in its aspects of hotel life and administration; or, in another sense, the forms that have been caused by a luminous thought to arise in sublimated expression of these needs in visible forms of beauty.

The true meaning of the word practical is completely elucidated in this structure. For "practical" signifies explicit and implicit human needs. Such needs run a wide gamut of desire, ranging from the immediately physical and material, gradually upward in series through the desires of emotional, intellectual and spiritual satisfactions.

Thus we can understand how important is the play of imagination; for imagination is distinct from intellect. It lies deeper in life, and uses intellect as a critical executive instrument wherewith to carry its visions of reality into reality itself, while determining its quality of procedure, at every stage. Otherwise intellect would dominate imagination, and pervert its ends.

Thus what we call art and what we call science are indissoluble within a masterful imagination. But imagination must be free to act in true accord with need and with desire as fundamental human traits; and intellect must be disciplined by the will to act in accord with imagination's fine desires. But for this initiative, and to this end, man's spirit must be free: unimpeded by irrelevant inhibitions. The vision of the free spirit ever seeks to clarify, to amplify what we call the commonplace. It sees within the so-called commonplace the elements of sublimity. Thus the architect who combines in his being the powers of vision, of imagination, of intellect, of sympathy with human need and the power to interpret them in a language vernacular and true—is he who shall create poems in stone, consonant with the finer clearing thought of our day, and the days of our expectancy.

In this regard the Imperial Hotel stands unique as the high water mark thus far attained by any modern architect. Superbly beautiful it stands— a noble prophecy.

REFLECTIONS ON THE TOKYO DISASTER

In my preceding article on the Imperial Hotel in Tokyo I prefaced by saying: "On the vast stage of the world drama, two ideas, both of them immense in power, confront each other in spectacular appeal to the fears and the courage of mankind." The casual reader, as a rule, is not accustomed to those generalizations which go under the—to him—somewhat repellent name of philosophy, and in so far as philosophy has dealt and deals solely with abstractions and nonentities, he is right in his disdain—which I share. Such philosophies as have gone by the names Platonic, Neo-Platonic, and German Transcendentalism, have done their huge share to fill the world with sorrow, for they and their kind are the intellectual basis of tyranny. And this same casual reader is as casually apt to be unaware that day by day he lives under the tyranny of abstract dehumanized ideas; that he is under the dominion of ideas he had no share in making, ideas so diaphanous and all-pervading that they are as the air he breathes. His disdain of philosophy therefore is but disdain of a word. Of the saturnine content of that word he is as unsuspecting as a kitten. If he is a university man, an aspirant in philosophy, he has been taught to revere that word and its content; and in innocence he reveres them both—and so another kitten, not in the least comprehending the utter heartlessness of it all; not in the least perceiving in the world about him the corruption and dislocation that have followed in its train. To be sure there are readers and readers. One reads industriously, and learns nothing—he is credulous. Another reads industriously and learns nothing—he is cynical. Another reads even more industriously and widely and learns nothing—he is pessimistic. But of all three and their varieties, the credulous one is in the most pitiful plight.

He may read the philosophies of abstraction and find them ennobling, he may believe himself to be lifted up and to have entered the highest attainable domain of pure thought—the realm of the ideal, the perfect, the absolute, in which the intellect reigns supreme—regarding itself in its own supernatural mirror, its gaze fatefully turned away from man and from his world. And of such belief in the unreal is the basis for all credulity—especially in evidence in the wool-gathering high-brow. Yet there is another class of reader—he who regards not authority, eminence, nor prestige as finalities, but who seeks that which nourishes and enlarges his comprehension of life, and who, therefore, as by instinct of self-preservation, rejects that which sterilizes life—that is to say the abstract. To him therefore Life becomes an ever broadening, deepening, sublimating and impressive flow, within which he finds himself moving—his own life unfolding, and with the passing years thus arises, within, a deep religious and moral sympathy with the vast spectacle of immediate life, enfolding mankind, which he envisages as participant and spectator. In sympathy there arises within, a new pity allied to a new faith in man.

With spontaneous gesture the newly-arising philosophy, with the voice of which I speak, sweeps aside the spooks and phantasms which have tyrannized the credulous and made slaves of high and low, even in our own day of so-called enlightenment, and with mind thus cleared for action and merging with the flow of life seeks therein a comprehension of mankind, in order to arrive at an outline of conservation, which, in its directness of purpose, may supersede the abominable wastage of humanity due to the prevailing confusion of ideas.

In one aspect the eye views an incredibly frantic industry, with no objective but to sell, and in another aspect—an inexorable reaction of the first—a steady decline in thought beyond the immediate frenzy, a terrifying inability to foresee the consequences of a thought or an act; or worse, a wanton and brutal disregard. And while it is a fact that the thoughts here above set down arise immediately out of contemplation of the helplessness, the shabbiness, the ruthless debauchery of commercialized American architecture—which means death—the same thought reaches out over the world and crossing the wide waters arrives at Japan with its city of Tokyo, in which has been staged, as but yesterday, a startling tragedy of ideas, wherein the abstract has crumbled in universal ruin, while one living thought and living thing survives. This is what is involved in the significance of the statement that on the vast stage of the world-drama two ideas, both of them immense in power, confront each other in spectacular appeal to the fears and the courage of mankind.

The emergence, unharmed, of the Imperial Hotel, from the heartrending horrors of the Tokyo disaster, takes on, at once, momentous importance in the world of modern thought, as a triumph of the living and the real over the credulous, the fantastic and the insane.

It emerges moreover before our gaze as an imposing upreared monument to the power of common sense; to that consummate common sense which perceives, comprehends, and grasps the so-called commonplace, the real, as distinct from the abstract; to that common sense which founds its logic upon the power inhering in nature's processes when interpreted in terms of action, as affecting results; soundly scientific in foreseeing results; and which towards this end employs an accurate imagination. For it requires unusual imagination to see stone as stone, brick as brick, wood as wood, steel as steel, the earth as the earth and human beings as human beings.

We may call this power inspiration if we please,

and if we think the word sounds pleasanter than Philosophy. But it is well to bear in mind that Inspiration is philosophy in its highest estate, and that true philosophy is systemized common sense in its finest human reach.

In planning the erection of a structure in a terrain habitually given to earthquake it would seem to be natural to regard earthquake—otherwise seismic disturbance—as a fundamental. For earthquakes are not imaginary or abstract or illusory; they are real—and at times calamitous. It would seem, therefore, to be but the part of common sense not to invite destruction. Yet such is the pervading American credulity, such its inability to think straight; such its impulsive acceptance of "go-gettism" and "pep" and "progress" and "enterprise" as substitutes for reflection and sound thought, and social responsibility, that it succeeded by sales-methods in imposing upon the Japanese, structures so childish, so absurd, so uncomprehending, as verily to invite destruction. To be sure the Japanese themselves were credulous enough to take the bait of boosted land values, and multiplied areas; and in their cupidity were induced to hold the bag. When the time came they found the bag filled not with purring kittens, but with terrifying wild-cats.

Prior to the American invasion, there has been an English invasion; and prior to the English, a German invasion, both invasions carrying with them the sophisticated credulity of European culture. Both of these alien cultures erected solid masonry buildings upon earthquake land. When the time came, these structures groaned, and buried their dead.

Now, further, Japanese society being heaviest at the top, it would seem but in keeping that its indigenous structures, designed in the native idiom, built on narrow and tortuous lanes, should also be topheavy. When the time came the flying heavy roof tiles did their share in the general slaughter, and as well the flimsy bridges and the flimsiness in general. Thus ruined Tokyo became the prey of conflagration. Thus death arose out of the temblor and spread forth its arms over Tokyo doomed by a false premise.

It may seem quite easy to draw conclusions after the fact. If you really think so, try your hand on the European war. Or, make a diagnosis of contemporary American architecture. Or attempt an analysis of the American mind, tracing its activities back to their common source. These are, all of them, matters after the fact.

We are now to deal with the reverse aspect of the problem. That is to say, with the primary assumption of earthquake and disaster, and how to forefend. Some five years prior to the now historic temblor a young man of forty seven was called to Tokyo to consult as architect regarding the planning and construction of a great hotel to be called the "Imperial". This man, a poet, who had reduced thinking to simples, began his solution with the fixed fact of earthquakes as a basis and made an emotional study of their nature and movements. The second move was the resolve never to relax his grip on the basic fact of earthquake as a menace, and to devise a system of construction such as should absorb and dispose of the powerful shocks, waves and violent tremors, and yet maintain its integrity as a fabricated structure. It may be remarked in passing, that the quality and power of emotion dramatizes the power of thought; that the poet is he whose thought, thus enriched, imparts telling power to the simple and the obvious, bringing them into the field of vivid consciousness.

It is precisely this power of the poet to bring earthquake vividly into consciousness and hold it there, that distinguishes him, in this instance, from the uninspired engineer. The latter is an extremely useful person, wherever and whenever his formulas, his slide-rule, his tables and his precedents—to which he is a slave—apply. Within the limits of routine he may successfully vary his processes in application; and there his social value ends. The same, in substance, may be said of the uninspired practicing architect, except that the latter, in addition, is invertebrate. Wherever he thinks with reasonable clearness, he approaches the engineer; but he is not a Yea-Sayer—he prefers to trim. Yet the great creative engineer—and there have been such—by virtue of clear eyesight, material realization and the power to dream, is again the poet if he fail not in the human sense of beauty, even though he may not think so, and out of prudence may not say so. Yet he is essentially of the Yea-Sayers—and the Yea-Sayers are the great modern poets.

The architect of the Imperial Hotel, whose name by the way is Frank Lloyd Wright, a fact I should in all honor have mentioned earlier, had I not been so engrossed in an attempt to clothe in words the basic idea of my thesis—the most dangerous and destructive of all ideas—the idea of Credulity; this architect I say, whom I have known since his eighteenth year, and the workings of whose fine mind I believe I fairly follow, is possessed of a rare sense of the human, and an equally rare sense of Mother Earth, coupled with an apprehension of the material, so delicate as to border

on the mystic, and yet remain coördinate with those facts we call real life. Such mind, sufficiently enriched by inner experiences as to become mellow in power, and reinforced by a strong tenacious will, is precisely the primary type of mind that resolves a problem into its simples, and out of these simples projects in thought a masterful solution, and in the process of transmuting thought into actual material fact, displays a virtuosity in the manipulation of the simples of technique.

I admit it is difficult for a mind academically trained and hence in large measure deprived of its freedom and its natural susceptibility, to grasp an idea so foreign to its heritage of tradition as is, necessarily so, the idea of simples. I go further and assert that such idea may be repugnant to such minds—may even alarm such minds—it is too disturbing in its ominous suggestion that thoughts may be living things—Now!—Here!— The intrusion of Life upon such minds may indeed be disheartening. And the same statements may apply with equal force to the mind technically trained exclusively—the world of life shut out; and as well to the business mind, with its airy system of phantasies, its curious rules of the game, its pontifical utterances of the higher wisdom of mendacity, and its one, solid, credulous faith in the abstract notion, deeply cherished, that human life is and must ever be a battle, a struggle for existence, and thus believing render itself "the unfit" to analyze its own symptoms which predicate periodical collapse of the structure it has reared upon the soil of an earthquake thought. And yet, in contrast, the open mind which may have won its freedom through valor, going forth into the world of men and thoughts and things, discerns basic simples everywhere and in all things. To such mind the confusion of the world is no mystery.

It is no part of my business here, nor of my intent, to go into the technical refinements, the subtleties of reaction, and the plastic sense of balance and free movement that enter into the structural theory and actuality of the Imperial Hotel. Mr. Wright may do this if he so sees fit. The vast sumptuous building, in all its aspects: structural, utilitarian and aesthetic, was the embodiment, and is now the revelation, of a single thought tenaciously held by a seer and a prophet, a craftsman, a master-builder.

This most significant architectural monument that the modern world can show, stands today uninjured because it was thought-built, so to stand. It was not and is not an imposition upon the Japanese, but a free will contribution to the finest elements of their culture. The fame of the building and its author is now world-wide; and we will let it go at that.

Meanwhile, I declare as my real business and my true intent herein, to be that of one of enquiring mind who seeks in this disaster the realities behind its terrifying mask.